HIT LIST

Taking Aim at the Seven Deadly Sins

Brian G. Hedges
Cruciform Press | November 2014

D0555689

To Tim Smith

CruciformPress

"*Hit List* is a great book! Hedges brings the historic framework of the seven deadly sins into the 21st century. Brian's reading and research into historic Christian theology enriches this readable and thoroughly biblical examination and treatment of 'the big seven.'"

Tedd Tripp, author, conference speaker

"Satan destroys by cloaking his schemes in darkness. *Hit List* is a blazing floodlight—both convicting and gleaming with gospel clarity. For the Christian soldier eager to win the daily war against sin, *Hit List* is a welcome field manual."

Alex Crain, Editor, Christianity.com

"With the exception of the Puritan John Owen, no other single author has helped me to understand the mortification of sin like Brian Hedges has. Brian, himself an avid reader of Owen, gives readers a clear picture not simply of the sinfulness of sin, but of the real means to fighting it, namely the gospel. This short book is packed with the rich theology, practical wisdom, and probing questions needed to make it useful for both personal growth and biblical counseling. I will be making use of it for years."

Dave Dunham, Associate Pastor of Discipleship and Counseling, Cornerstone Baptist Church

"Brian Hedges goes where few dare to go: He takes on the classic seven deadly sins in *Hit List*, and does not just biblically explain them well, but also gives theologically solid and practically insightful gospel solutions for them. This author's refined writing style and pastoral wisdom, which measures well beyond his years, oozes from this entire book. For those desiring a pastoral guide through these often misunderstood root sins that will leave you fixed upon the cross of Christ, you have found the right man and the right book for the task."

Brian Croft, author; Senior Pastor, Auburndale Baptist Church; Founder, Practical Shepherding

"Quick quiz for you: Do you know how to distinguish between sinful anger and righteous anger? Do you know what's at the root of your pride every single time? How about the surprising cures for gluttony? *Hit List* includes answers to all these questions and so much more. It's not just an academic read, though. Brian includes application questions at the end of each chapter because none of us are immune to the disease of sin. If you've ever heard you shouldn't envy (or get angry or lust or ...), but you don't know exactly what those sins look like in your everyday life—let alone the cure—then *Hit List* is for you. Brian has done his research, and I'm personally grateful for his insights on what's at the root of specific sins I deal with...and how I can break free. Read, repent, and live free!"

Paula Hendricks, Writing & Editorial Manager, Revive Our Hearts; author of *Confessions of a Boy-Crazy Girl: On Her Journey from Neediness to Freedom*

"We live in a culture in which spirituality is on the rise, including a resurgence in mysticism, Gnosticism, and every other -ism. Many are confused about what they believe and why it matters, and sin is often minimized or hidden. Hedges draws on the best wisdom of the church to help readers better grasp the seven deadly sins and how the gospel frees God's people from them. As *Hit List* blows away misconceptions about the sinfulness of man, readers will be captivated by the magnificence of what Jesus has done so sinners can put their sin to death and grow in the grace of God. This is an excellent and needed book. It can convict you of your sinfulness while pointing you to the sufficiency of the finished work of the Savior—Jesus Christ."

Dave Jenkins, Executive Director, Servants of Grace Ministries; Executive Editor, *Theology for Life*

"If you're dying from a disease, of course you want to understand what's killing you. But even more than diagnosis, you want a cure. With characteristic depth, Brian unpacks an ancient formulation of our soul-sickness, while giving us the antidote of grace and gospel. This book is medicine for the soul!"

Del Fehsenfeld III, Senior Editor, *Revive* magazine

"This is a clear, vivid, insightful introduction to the seven deadly sins. Hedges argues convincingly that reflection on the capital vices—and the virtues that fight them—is central to Christian spiritual formation. *Hit List* is a richly rewarding read."

Nathan King, Philosophy Department, Whitworth University

CruciformPress

<u>Our Books:</u> Short and to the point—about 100 pages.
Clear. Concise. Helpful. Inspiring. Easy to read.
Solid authors. Gospel-focused. Local-church oriented.

<u>Website Discounts:</u>

Print Books (list price $9.99)

1-5 Books	$8.45 each
6-50 Books	$7.45 each
More than 50 Books	$6.45 each

Ebooks (list price $7.50)

Single Ebooks	$5.45 each
Bundles of 7 Ebooks	$35.00
Ebook Distribution Program	6 pricing levels

<u>Subscription Options:</u> If you choose, print books or
ebooks delivered to you on a schedule, at a discount.

Print Book Subscription *(list $9.99)*	$6.49 each
Ebook Subscription *(list $7.50)*	$3.99 each

Hit List: Taking Aim at the Seven Deadly Sins

Print / PDF ISBN: 978-1-936760-98-5
ePub ISBN: 978-1-936760-66-4
Mobipocket ISBN: 978-1-936760-99-2

Table of Contents

FOREWORD

The evangelical church in our day desperately needs to recover a more biblically informed understanding of the nature of human sinfulness. I'm concerned that many people we know who claim to be followers of Jesus are deceived about the condition of their soul and their eternal destiny because they have failed to understand what the Bible teaches us about the deceitfulness and wickedness of the human heart apart from the transforming grace of God.

I believe this in part because I spent years deceived about the condition of my own soul until someone explained the reality of my sin to me in a way I had never heard it explained before.

For several years in my late teens and early twenties, I had what I now see was a superficial and not a saving knowledge of Jesus. During this time, I attended church each week. During my college years, I met with local high school students regularly, doing evangelism and discipleship. I thought I was a Christian because I had done what people had told me I needed to do. I had bowed my head and prayed the prayer. I had confessed with my mouth that Jesus is Lord and believed in my heart that God raised Him from the dead.

One summer, following a Bible study with other

college students, I was approached by someone in our group who asked if he could meet with me later that week. He said he had some questions he wanted to ask me. I agreed to meet, thinking that I must have somehow impressed him with my wisdom and insight into the Bible during our discussion. My first impulse of pride and arrogance should have been a tip off that I had not yet been humbled and tamed by the gospel.

When we met, the questions my friend had for me were about my understanding of Romans 3. He opened his Bible and asked me to read and explain vv 10–18, where the Apostle Paul pulls from a number of Old Testament passages to describe the deep rooted nature of human sinfulness. "There is none righteous, no not one," Paul writes. I had read that passage before, thinking it might have indeed been true about the people to whom Paul was writing, but never stopping to consider that this passage was describing me.

I remember walking away from that meeting that day feeling weak in the knees and a bit disoriented. I felt like I had been punched in the gut. I felt confused. I was like a patient who had gone to the doctor for a routine physical only to learn that in spite of a lack of any kind of symptoms, he was suffering from a terminal and incurable disease and did not have long to live.

My understanding of my sin prior to that meeting was that I had "missed the mark" or "fallen short." Because of my pride, what I heard in those definitions was that I had "come close" and "hit the target, but missed the bulls-eye." I saw myself as a mostly good, mostly moral, mostly righteous person who needed a Savior to take care of the relatively few minor infractions in my life.

This seeker sensitive description of my sinfulness was one of the things that had kept me from really crying out for God to save me. I had asked Jesus to pay my debts. I just thought we were talking about pocket change, not life change.

Romans 3, and later other biblical texts, helped me see more clearly the totality of my depravity. By God's grace, I was now able to see that what God had to say about the condition of my heart was truer than what I believed. I began to see that when we talk about the fall of mankind, we're not talking about a slip or a stumble. We're talking about corruption and treason and rebellion.

After taking me to Romans 3, my friend did not walk me through an evangelistic tract. He didn't lead me in a prayer to "give my heart to Jesus." He simply showed me what the Bible says about the depth of my sin, and he showed me what the Bible says about the cure: asking God to save me by His grace and replace my hard, dead heart with a new one. I finally understood the good news because for the first time in my life, I had begun to really understand the bad news.

I am grateful that Brian Hedges has tackled the subject of our sin, first in his very helpful book *Licensed to Kill*, and now in *Hit List*. His previous work addresses our need to mortify and not attempt to manage our sin. He gives wise, pastoral counsel on how we can "put to death what is earthly" in us. This new volume provides the same kind of helpful guidance. You will want to wear steel toed boots as you read. Be prepared to wince.

The comic strip character Pogo, the swamp dwelling possum who appeared daily in newspapers for more than 25 years, is best known for having declared "We have met the enemy, and it is us." How true. Your greatest enemy is not outside of you, but inside of you. You will not like the description that follows. But reading what Brian Hedges has written will help you know your enemy. And the better you know him, the more prepared you will be for the battle ahead.

Bob Lepine
Co-Host, FamilyLife Today
Pastor, Redeemer Community Church of Little Rock

One
THE BIG SEVEN

The Christian life is a war and one of your most lethal enemies hangs its helmet inside your heart.

This infernal, internal enemy is sin, which even after new birth continues to reside in every believer. As followers of Jesus, we've been given a simple mission regarding sin: search and destroy. Put it to death. The old word for this is *mortification*. I wrote about mortification in *Licensed to Kill* a book about the dynamics of sin and temptation, the holy violence required in the battle against sin, and the sin-killing power of Christ's cross, Word, and Spirit.[1]

But in the words of Cornelius Plantinga Jr., "sin has a thousand faces."[2] It is one thing to oppose sin in principle, quite another to actually do the bloody work of crucifying specific sin patterns in our lives. Sometimes these patterns are difficult to detect. Always they fight back, tooth and nail, mounting vehement resistance in counter-maneuvers of a variety and complexity that would send General Schwarzkopf's mind spinning like a tilt-a-whirl.

The most famous faces of sin are the Seven Deadly Sins: pride, envy, wrath, sloth, greed, gluttony, and lust. The list is centuries old, found as frequently in literature and pop culture as in manuals of theology and devotion.

Dante surveyed these sins in his tours through hell and purgatory in *The Divine Comedy*, Chaucer moralized about them in "The Parson's Tale," and Brad Pitt investigated a series of grisly murders based on the list in *Se7en*.

On my first mission trip to Africa I quickly learned about the "Big Five"—the lion, elephant, rhinoceros, leopard, and Cape buffalo—the most difficult game to hunt on foot, and also the five animals you hope to see on a safari. The deadly sins are the Big Seven among our moral and spiritual foes.

They are the leading undercover operatives for the world, the flesh, and the devil, that evil complex of powers arrayed against our souls. And while we may recognize these sins by their names, we are often misled by the subtlety of their methods and ways. Like the super spies in *Mission Impossible*, these sins are masters of disguise, adept at masking their true nature in charades of harmlessness, acceptability, and fun. If *Licensed to Kill* was a field manual for how to kill sin, *Hit List* provides detailed dossiers on seven of our most dangerous enemies.

But why study this list? After all, these sins are never grouped together in Scripture. You also might wonder about some of the sins that *don't* make the list, like lying, stealing, and adultery. Heck, even murder isn't on the list. Aren't those sins worse than gluttony and sloth? Why did this particular group of seven get included? And where did the list come from anyway? Isn't this a Roman Catholic thing?

The Origin of the List

It's true that the Big Seven are never grouped together in the Bible. But that alone is hardly a reason not to study them. After all, the Scriptures never use the word Trinity, provide a single detailed list of spiritual disciplines, or outline in one place the doctrines of grace. Yet many readers will recognize the instructive value of these extra-biblical categories and frameworks because, rightly used, they can aid our accurate understanding of Scripture.

And while the list of seven is recognized by the Roman Catholic church, its origin actually dates back to the fourth century. The first person to give us such a list was a monk in the Eastern tradition named Evagrius of Pontus. In his treatise *On the Eight Thoughts*, Evagrius listed eight evil thoughts or "demons" that hound and harass the desert hermit. Evagrius' work is basically a catalog of problems and temptations faced by the monk, each followed by a lengthy list of biblical passages to use in resistance.[3]

In the following generation, one of Evagrius' students, John Cassian, wrote more extensively on these eight sins, organizing them into categories of natural and unnatural (by which he meant those which "cannot be consummated without bodily action, such as gluttony and fornication," and others that "can be completed without any bodily action whatsoever, such as pride and vainglory"), and showing how one sin feeds into another.[4] But it was Gregory the Great, hailed by Calvin as the "*last* bishop of Rome,"[5] who condensed the list to seven in his late sixth century treatise *Morals on the Book of Job*.[6]

The Value of the List

The various names and models for understanding the list of seven lend insight into its value. The most common designation, of course, is the one I've already used: seven *deadly* sins. On one level we can agree these sins are deadly, because Scripture clearly teaches that the "wages of sin is death" (Romans 6:23). But this is true of all sins, not just the seven that made the list. In Roman Catholic theology, a "deadly sin" is a *mortal* sin that destroys charity, the principle of grace in the heart, in contrast to a *venial* sin that only wounds and weakens charity, but does not destroy it.[7] I don't accept this distinction between mortal and venial as biblical, partly because all sins in their nature are deadly, not just a select list. But more importantly, I think Roman Catholic doctrine misunderstands the nature of grace, for Scripture teaches that we are regenerated not merely by a principle of grace implanted in the heart, but by the indwelling of God's Spirit. And once the Spirit indwells believers, he will never leave them or forsake them, even though he may be grieved. We can, nevertheless, call these sins "deadly," for as John Mabray writes, "These seven are…'deadly' in the sense that they are sinful dispositions which, if given free reign, would take over our lives — spirit, soul, and body — and lead us further and further down the wide road of destruction (Matthew 7:13)."[8]

Capital Sins

I find even more helpful an older designation for the list of seven: the "capital sins." *Capital* comes from the Latin word for head, *caput*, meaning source, like the head of a river. These sins were considered capital sins not because they were the worst, but because they were gateway sins, what Dorothy Sayers called, "well-heads from which all sinful behavior ultimately springs…the *Seven Roots of Sinfulness*."[9]

John Cassian thus called them "principal vices,"[10] while Gregory the Great imagined them as military captains commanding entire armies of sins.[11] As Rebecca Konyndyk DeYoung notes in her excellent book, *Glittering Vices*, writers in the Middle Ages often compared the sins to a tree with its network of roots and branches. While pride was the root and trunk, the vices of vainglory, envy, wrath, sloth, avarice, gluttony, and lust were the main branches, out of which grew many other branches, each yielding a harvest of fatal fruit.[12] The seven, then, are leading sins, breeding sins that nest deeply in our hearts and engender whole broods of further sins.

Habitual Vices

But the seven sins should be viewed not only as capital sins, but also as deeply ingrained, character-shaping habits of the heart. This insight is captured by the language of virtue and vice. "Virtues," writes DeYoung, "are 'excellences' of character, habits, or dispositions of character that help us live well as human beings…Similarly, the vices are corruptive and destructive habits. They undermine both our goodness of character and our living and acting well."[13]

As the vise in your garage or workshop has the capacity to clench an object tightly in the grip of its mechanical jaws, so the seven vices tenaciously hold human beings in their grasp.

These vices are to be distinguished from sinful*ness* on the one hand, and single sinful acts on the other. "Vices concern deeply rooted patterns in our character, patterns broader than a single act but narrower than our sinful condition in general."[14] That is, one angry outburst does not in itself mean that wrath is your vice. But if you are as adept at unleashing hostile words as Indiana Jones is at lashing a whip, wrath has a nameplate on the door of your heart.

Vices don't take hold overnight. Instead, they "are gradually internalized and become firm and settled through years of formation."[15] They are thus habitual sins, patterns woven deeply into the fabric of your disposition and temperament. Like Jacob Marley's chains in Dickens' *A Christmas Carol*, they are forged by our own choices and actions, one cruel link at a time. They encompass us, weigh us down, and follow us everywhere.

Therefore, this list of vices can also have diagnostic value. Studying the Big Seven can help us "to recognize and identify networks of sin in our lives and discover layers of sin of which we were previously unaware."[16]

Disordered Loves

Like all sin, these seven arise from our confused attempts to secure happiness apart from God.[17] Augustine wrote about "the sham, shadowy beauty with which even vice allures us" since even "in vice there lurks a counterfeit beauty." Augustine included numerous examples of how, in all our vices, we either imitate or seek out good things that can truly be found only in God. "A soul that turns away from you [God] therefore lapses into fornication when it seeks apart from you what it can never find in pure and limpid form except by returning to you. All those who wander far away and set themselves up against you are imitating you, but in a perverse way."[18]

Each one of our sins, in other words, is a case of misdirected, disordered love. This perspective was developed by later thinkers like Aquinas and Dante, but it's also a window into the biblical category of idolatry, for idols in Scripture aren't merely or mainly images of wood and stone, but substitutes for God himself, paramours we pursue with adulterous hearts when we've forsaken our Divine Lover.

That's why the prophet Jeremiah links idolatry with adultery and rebukes the people of God for seeking satisfaction in lesser gods. "Be appalled, O heavens, at this; be shocked, be utterly desolate, declares the LORD, for my people have committed two evils: they have forsaken me, the fountain of living waters, and hewed out cisterns for themselves, broken cisterns that can hold no water" (Jeremiah 2:12–13).

Seeing sin more clearly as the foolish and fatal attempt to find satisfaction apart from God should provoke both sorrow and hope in our hearts. Sorrow, when we realize our sins aren't mere peccadilloes but grievous offenses against the lover of our souls. But also hope, when we see that the thirst we sought to quench in broken cisterns is actually a yearning that God alone can satisfy.

C. S. Lewis, in one of his letters, likens our sins to a dog whose owner takes it on a walk with a leash. The dog goes on the opposite side of a pole from its owner and gets pulled up short. His owner knows the dog is stuck so he tries to pull him *back*, in order to take him *forward*. The dog wants the same thing as his owner: to walk forward. But he's trying to get it in a way that simply can't work.

So it is with us. The desire "which is at the root of all my evil," says Lewis, "is the desire for complete and ecstatic happiness." And this is exactly what God has made us for. "But he knows, and I do not, how it can be really and permanently attained. He knows that most of *my* personal attempts to reach it are actually putting it further and further out of my reach." We can therefore be rid of,

> the old haunting suspicion—which raises its head in every temptation—that there is something else than God…some kind of delight [which] he "doesn't appreciate" or just chooses to forbid, but which [would] be real delight if only we were allowed to get it. The thing *just isn't there.* Whatever we desire is either what God is trying to give us as quickly as he can, or else a false picture of what he is trying to give us—a false picture [which] would not attract us for a moment if we saw the real thing…he knows what we want, even in our vilest acts: he is longing to give it to us…Only because he has laid up *real* goods for us to desire are we able to go wrong by snatching at them in greedy, misdirected ways. The truth is that evil is not a real *thing* at all, like God. It is simply good *spoiled.* That is why I say there can be good without evil, but no evil without good. You know what the biologists mean by a parasite—an animal that lives on another animal. Evil is a *parasite.* It is there only because good is there for it to spoil and confuse.[19]

Deadly sins, capital sins, glittering vices, disordered loves, idolatry. We'll return to these categories in the following chapters as we examine these seven species of sin in more detail. But since the thought of taking on these sins may leave you feeling like a patient waiting to see an oncologist or Frodo on the edge of Mordor, a word of encouragement may be in order.

The Great Sovereign Remedy for Sin-Sick Souls

In my research of the deadly sins over the past couple of years, I have found that the ancient moral theologians of the church are helpful for diagnosis, but not always for cure. I'm too far removed from the monastic spirituality of the desert fathers to find them of great help. I'm not a cloistered hermit, but a busy pastor, husband, and father of four children. While I appreciate the scintillating intellect of Aquinas and the imaginative powers of Dante, I inhabit a different theological tradition than they, one that I believe is both more hopeful and more true to the Scriptures. In keeping with the tradition of the Reformers, the Puritans, and their heirs, it's my conviction that the only way to dismantle vices and mortify sin is with a strong dose of justification by faith alone and the heart-transforming ministry of the Holy Spirit.

John Owen, whose trilogy of books on mortification, temptation, and indwelling sin so deeply informed *Licensed to Kill*, said, "Mortification from a self-strength, carried on by ways of self-invention, unto the end of a self-righteousness, is the soul and substance of all false religion in the world."[20] Unfortunately, that's just the kind of moral advice given by many counselors both living and dead: a prescription of cognitive therapy, behavior modification, or religious practices that may result in superficial change, but essentially leave us to ourselves, with hearts untouched by the love of Christ and the grace of his Spirit.

But Scripture prescribes a better way.

> If then you have been raised with Christ, seek the things that are above, where Christ is, seated at the

right hand of God. Set your minds on things that are above, not on things that are on earth. For you have died, and your life is hidden with Christ in God. When Christ who is your life appears, then you also will appear with him in glory. Put to death therefore what is earthly in you. (Colossians 3:1–5a)

If the Spirit of him who raised Jesus from the dead dwells in you, he who raised Christ Jesus from the dead will also give life to your mortal bodies through his Spirit who dwells in you. So then, brothers, we are debtors, not to the flesh, to live according to the flesh. For if you live according to the flesh you will die, but if by the Spirit you put to death the deeds of the body, you will live. For all who are led by the Spirit of God are sons of God. (Romans 8:11–14)

Killing sin isn't *simply* a matter of exercising greater will power. It's not less than that, of course, but it is far more. For the only effective way to mortify sin is to draw on the resources that are already ours through our union with Christ in his death and resurrection. Then, with the confident security of God's grace beneath us, the solid hope of glory before us, and the power of his Spirit within us, we can enter the fray. No, we won't achieve perfection. But we don't have to, for Christ's obedience is already ours. The war is already won. "'It is finished'" (John 19:30).

This means we can fight with confidence, knowing we're already accepted in Christ and someday we will be fully conformed to his glorious image once and for all. And this means real change is possible now, even as the battle continues. Therefore, my friend, "*Set faith at*

work on Christ for the killing of your sin. His blood is
the great sovereign remedy for sin-sick souls. Live in this,
and you will die a conqueror; yea, you will, through the
good providence of God, live to see your lust dead at your
feet."[21]

Examine and Apply

1. What was your perspective on the seven deadly sins
   before reading this chapter? Do you see more value
   to the list now than before?
2. What patterns of sin do you see in your own life?
   Could these patterns indicate the presence of vice in
   your character?
3. When you think about sin as a disordered love
   or misguided attempt to find satisfaction, does it
   provoke sadness, hope, or both?
4. How does the good news of Christ's finished work
   change your approach to fighting sin?

Two
PRIDE

One driving conviction of this book is that all our moral, behavioral, and relational problems are really the results of much deeper spiritual issues.[22] The church fathers understood this and drew on the familiar biblical imagery of roots and fruits to teach it. They knew that our sinful habit patterns were the fruits of deeper spiritual roots. And they believed that the deepest root of all is pride.

That's why Gregory the Great, the first theologian to give us a distinctive list of seven sins, wrote,

> For pride is the root of all evil . . . But seven principal vices, as its first progeny, spring doubtless from this poisonous root, namely, vainglory, envy, anger, melancholy, avarice, gluttony, lust. For, because he grieved that we were held captive by these seven sins of pride, therefore our Redeemer came to the spiritual battle of our liberation, full of the spirit of sevenfold grace.[23]

In later lists, the vice of vainglory was subsumed under pride, and the vice of melancholy gave way to the sin of sloth. But theologians through the centuries have agreed with Gregory's conviction that pride is the root of all evil, "the queen of sins."[24]

C. S. Lewis called pride "the great sin." "According to Christian teachers," he said, "the essential vice, the utmost evil, is Pride. Unchastity, anger, greed, drunkenness, and all that, are mere fleabites in comparison . . . Pride leads to every other vice."[25] In Proverbs 8:13, pride and arrogance top the list of sins that God hates. And Proverbs 16:18 reminds us, "Pride goes before destruction, and a haughty spirit before a fall." Whenever and wherever sin wreaks its havoc in human lives, you can be sure that pride is at the root.

To grasp this root/fruit imagery in practice, we'll explore three connected topics in this chapter: the fruits of pride, the deep root of pride itself, and how the gospel equips us to kill the root sin of pride.

The Fruits of Pride

On one level, the fruits of pride are almost beyond counting. We'll look at many of these sins in later chapters, but there are three common fruits of pride that demand closer attention here: self-promotion, self-pity, and self-righteousness.

Self-Promotion

Self-promotion is perhaps the most obvious. Of course, there are times when it is necessary to refer to one's accomplishments or credentials—when seeking employment, for example. But there is a sinful kind of self-promotion as well: a vice that repels us when we see it in others, but are often blind to in ourselves. Think of the guy who is always name-dropping at a party, or the woman whose dress is a bit too provocative, or the show-off on the basketball court, or the fresh college graduate flaunting his newly discovered knowledge. The biblical word for this is *boasting*. When Scripture targets pride, it often sets boasting in the crosshairs. "Thus says the LORD: 'Let not the *wise man boast* in his wisdom, let not the *mighty man boast* in his might, let not the *rich man boast* in his riches'" (Jeremiah 9:23).

Boasting was a huge problem in the Corinthian church, surfacing more than forty times in Paul's two Corinthian letters. Paul uses a vivid Greek word to describe boasting, a term "used to describe the pompous windbag"[26] that "suggests self-centered actions in which there is an inordinate desire to call attention to oneself."[27] Paul confronts this excessive self-promotion by showing the Corinthians that they have no grounds for boasting outside of the crucified Christ. Though we tend to boast in wealth, power, wisdom, knowledge, and spiritual experiences, God usually chooses not the wise, powerful, or noble of this world, but the foolish, weak, low, and despised, "so that no human being might boast in the presence of God" (1 Corinthians 1:26–29).

Like the Corinthians, we tend to boast in the wrong things. But when we are confronted with the stark realities of gospel grace, we learn that God doesn't broker on the basis of privilege, merit, or personal success. Grace comes through faith in Christ's finished work alone. And faith excludes boasting (Romans 3:27).

Self-Pity

"That doesn't describe me at all," you might respond. "I don't ever boast in those kinds of things. I'm never guilty of self-promotion. I don't boast in my wisdom, because I don't feel smart. I don't boast in my might or my beauty, because I'm not athletic or beautiful. I don't boast in my riches, because I don't make a lot of money." And you might therefore conclude that pride isn't your issue, that you can just skip the rest of this chapter and move on to the next.

Not so fast.

Your pride may just be wearing a different mask: not self-promotion, but self-pity. I don't mean the whimpering "poor me" kind of self-pity (though that also qualifies). I mean the subtle insecurity and self-consciousness that we often feel in comparison with others. When we hold up that arrogant boaster as the primary example of pride, we can imagine he is the *only* example. But pride, as we will see in the next section, is all about excessive self-focus; it can appear in many forms. We shouldn't be surprised that it manifests itself differently in people with different kinds of personalities and giftings.

Test yourself now. Do you ever feel uncomfortable around those more educated than you? Do you avoid participation in games or sports out of fear of looking stupid? Do you secretly criticize people who are more physically attractive? Are you excessively shy, even unfriendly? Are you afraid of what people think of you?

These things are also manifestations of pride, appearing not as conceit, but self-pity. John Piper offers helpful clarifications.

> Boasting is the response of pride to success. Self-pity is the response of pride to suffering. Boasting says, "I deserve admiration because I have achieved so much."

Self-pity says, "I deserve admiration because I have sacrificed so much." Boasting is the voice of pride in the heart of the strong. Self-pity is the voice of pride in the heart of the weak. Boasting sounds self-sufficient. Self-pity sounds self-sacrificing.

The reason self-pity does not look like pride is that it appears to be needy. But the need arises from a wounded ego and the desire of the self-pitying is not really for others to see them as helpless, but as heroes. The need self-pity feels does not come from a sense of unworthiness, but from a sense of unrecognized worthiness. It is the response of unapplauded pride."[28]

Self-Righteousness

But the most subtle and insidious fruit of pride is self-righteousness. Jesus told the powerful parable of the Pharisee and tax collector to expose and censure those "who trusted in themselves that they were righteous and treated others with contempt" (Luke 18:9).

Two men went up into the temple to pray, one a Pharisee and the other a tax collector. The Pharisee, standing by himself, prayed thus: "God, I thank you that I am not like other men, extortioners, unjust, adulterers, or even like this tax collector. I fast twice a week; I give tithes of all that I get." But the tax collector, standing far off, would not even lift up his eyes to heaven, but beat his breast, saying, "God, be merciful to me, a sinner!" I tell you, this man went down to his house justified, rather than the other. For everyone who exalts himself will be humbled, but the one who humbles himself will be exalted. (Luke 18:10–14)

I'll never forget a conversation one Sunday after my father preached on this passage. A group of men were standing just outside the church following the service, and the old patriarch deacon of the church was talking to Dad. This deacon must have been in his seventies, a weathered rough-hewn rancher of the Texas Big Country. He was a good man in many ways—honest, faithful, hardworking, and a stalwart in the church and community. He and Dad were talking about the sermon, and I heard him say, "Brother Ronnie, I'm so glad I'm not like that Pharisee."

I couldn't believe it! I picked my jaw up off the ground. How could he have missed the whole point of the sermon? By identifying himself with the tax collector and thinking he was better than the Pharisee, he had become just as self-righteous as the Pharisee himself. Unbelievable!

I'm sure glad I'm not like that deacon.

As you can see, pride is subtle. We can easily see its fruits in others, but fail to detect it in ourselves. Be sure of this: if you don't think you're proud, you are. And if you're starting to feel slightly gratified that you have the humility to recognize and admit your pride, watch out! The fruits of pride are there, whether you see them or not.

The Deep Root of Pride

Having looked at some of the fruits of pride, what is the root? If self-promotion, self-pity, and self-righteousness are various masks pride can wear, what is its true face?

The simple answer is *self*.

Pride is self-centeredness, self-concern, inordinate self-love. Cornelius Plantinga Jr. defines pride as "a blend of self-absorption—that is, narcissism—with an overestimate of one's abilities or worth—that is, conceit. So a proud person thinks a lot *about* herself and also thinks a lot *of* herself."[29] This is a helpful working definition of pride. *Pride is thinking much about one's self and much of one's self.* To borrow words from Augustine, pride is "the love of self, even to the contempt of God."[30]

The effect of inordinate self-love is provocatively illustrated in a little-known short story by C. S. Lewis called "The Shoddy Lands." Lewis himself narrates the story, which begins when Durward, a former student, comes to his office, accompanied by his fiancée, a young woman named Peggy. But as Lewis visits with the couple, he is transported out of his office into a strange and awful world. It is a world in which nearly everything—sky, trees, grass, flowers, people—is blurred and indistinct. Lewis finds it all terrifying.

> The full astonishment of my adventure was now beginning to descend on me. With it came fear, but, even more, a sort of disgust. I doubt if it can be fully conveyed to anyone who has not had a similar experience. I felt as if I had suddenly been banished from the real, bright, concrete, and prodigally complex world into some sort of second-rate universe that had all been put together on the cheap; by an imitator.

But then he sees daffodils, "real daffodils, trim and cool and perfect." And every now and then, "a face, a hat, or a dress would stand out in full detail." But the distinct clothes were always women's clothes, while the distinct faces were always men's faces. Then he passes by a jeweler's store and "everything in that window was perfect; every facet on every diamond distinct, every brooch and tiara finished down to the last perfection of intricate detail."

Finally he sees something so large that at first he thinks it's a building. He is shocked to discover it is a gigantic woman, the only distinct human shape he has seen in this place. Pretty soon it becomes clear that the giant woman is Peggy, the woman sitting in the room with his old student. It is her, but changed. Her physical attributes are improved: perfect teeth, perfect figure, fuller lips. "The complexion was so perfect that it suggested a very expensive doll." But though the morphed physical attributes made her look "exactly like the girl in all the advertisements," there was less kindness and honesty in her face than the original Peggy.

As Lewis continues his story, he eventually becomes aware of two noises that sound like knockings: "patient knockings, infinitely remote, as if two outsiders, two excluded people, were knocking on the walls of that world."

> The one was faint, but hard; and with it came a voice saying, "Peggy, Peggy, let me in." Durward's voice, I thought. But how shall I describe the other knocking? It was, in some curious way, soft; "soft as wool and sharp as death," soft but unendurably heavy, as if at each blow some enormous hand fell on the outside of the Shoddy Sky and covered it completely. And with that knocking came a voice at whose sound my bones turned to water: "Child, child, child, let me in before the night comes."

As those last words are uttered daylight rushes in upon him and Lewis is suddenly transported back to the real world, the concrete world of distinct physical objects in his room, with the couple sitting before him. And then he explains what must have happened to him:

> My view is that by the operation of some unknown psychological—or pathological—law, I was, for a second or two let into Peggy's mind; at least to the extent of seeing her world, the world as it exists for her. At the centre of that world is a swollen image of herself, remodeled to be as like the girls in the advertisements as possible. Round this are grouped clear and distinct images of the things she really cares about. Beyond that, the whole earth and sky are a vague blur. The daffodils and roses are especially instructive. Flowers only exist for her if they are the sort that can be cut and put in vases or sent in bouquets; flowers in themselves, flowers as you see them in the woods, are negligible.[31]

Lewis' story is as stimulating as it is fantastical: an insightful parable of the doleful emptiness of a self-centered life. A soul bent in on itself, worshiping self, rather than God. Such a life is small, its world dull, shoddy, and mostly uninteresting and gray.

But this inordinate love of self not only leaves the soul empty and dull, it is also hellish to the core. Lewis again provides the best illustration in *The Great Divorce*, where hell is portrayed as a gigantic grey city where miserable, self-absorbed, joyless ghosts live isolated lives, inhabiting lonely dwellings separated from others by hundreds of miles, because they can't stand each other. When a busload of the hellish wraiths take a furlough to the borderland of heaven, almost all of them turn away from the splendor, beauty, and joy because they will not give up their self-centered wills. "There are only two kinds of people in the world," Lewis observes, "those who say to God, 'Thy will be done.' And those to whom God says, in the end, '*Thy* will be done.'"[32] As Peter Kreeft quips, "The song they all sing in Hell is the hymn to pride: 'I Did It My Way.'"[33]

The irony of pride is that its very self-centeredness is also self-destructive. Christianity teaches that God created the human self with the capacity for infinite joy, but that such joy is only found through self-giving love. The true self, the whole self, is the self that is outward in its orientation, radiating love to God and others. But pride causes the self to collapse in on itself. "Sin as a *state of being* is the ultimate black hole of the spirit, the implosion of an inwardly gravitating self. The black hole is pride."[34]

How to Kill the Root

If the root of pride is self-centeredness to the exclusion of God and others, then how do we kill this root?

First, *we need to be humbled*. If pride is the root of all sins, then humility is the root of all virtues. Calvin called humility "the sovereign virtue….the mother and root of all virtue."[35] Jonathan Edwards said that humility was "the most essential thing in true religion."[36] When Bernard of Clairvaux was asked what the four cardinal virtues were, he replied, "Humility, humility, humility, and humility.'"[37]

But note that I'm not simply saying we need humility, but that we need to *be humbled*. Of course, we should humble ourselves. But the kind of humility we need isn't the result of will power, but the reflex of a heart captured by the vision of God. As John Owen said, "There are two things that are suited to humble the souls of men, and they are, first, a due consideration of God, and then of themselves—of *God*, in his greatness, glory, holiness, power, majesty, and authority; of *ourselves*, in our mean, abject, and sinful condition."[38]

These two things usually come together. Do you remember Isaiah's response to the stunning vision of the enthroned majesty and holiness of God in the temple? "And I said: 'Woe is me! For I am lost; for I am a man of unclean lips, and I dwell in the midst of a people of unclean lips; for my eyes have seen the King, the LORD of hosts!'" (Isaiah 6:5). Or think of Job, who after glimpsing the inscrutable wisdom and august power of God, confessed, "I had heard of you by the hearing of the ear, but now my eye sees you; therefore I despise myself, and repent in dust and ashes" (Job 42:5–6).

Humility flows from this double awareness of God's glorious holiness and our spiritual poverty. When we've been humbled, we become less consumed with ourselves. When our hearts are captured by the radiance of God's beauty and the glory of his holiness, we are less inclined to boast in ourselves, less concerned with what people think of us, and less prone to think we are better than others. The cancerous sins of self-promotion, self-pity, and self-righteousness will begin to wither and die in the radiation of God's glory.

But we not only need to be humbled, *we need to boast in something better*. Our hearts are glory vacuums, and we will only escape the gravitational pull of our inwardly imploding selves if there is a more powerful force holding our hearts in orbit. That's why the counsel of Scripture isn't only, "do not boast," but also "boast in the Lord" (See Psalm 34:2; Jeremiah 9:23–24; 1 Corinthians 1:26–31).

Is not the most effective way of bridling my delight in being made much of, to focus on making much of God? Self-denial and crucifixion of the flesh are essential, but O how easy it is to be made much of even for my self-denial! How shall this insidious motive of pleasure in being made much of be broken except through bending all my faculties to delight in the pleasure of making much of God![39]

The great secret to humility is not to focus on yourself at all, but to fill your mind and heart with the glory of God revealed in the sin-conquering death and resurrection of Jesus Christ.

> *I take, O cross, thy shadow for my abiding place;*
> *I ask no other sunshine than the sunshine of His face;*
> *Content to let the world go by to know no gain or loss,*
> *My sinful self my only shame, my glory all the cross.*[40]

Examine and Apply

1. Are you more prone to self-promotion or self-pity?
2. What are some evidences of self-righteousness in your life? Do you tend to look down on people who are more outwardly sinful than you? Do you cast judgment on judgmental people?
3. Can you think of other manifestations of pride not directly addressed in this chapter? Do you think you are proud?
4. How does boasting in Christ and his cross cultivate humility and undermine pride?

Three
ENVY

One of my favorite filmmakers is Christopher Nolan, director of *The Dark Knight* trilogy. One of his earlier films, *The Prestige*, is the story of Robert Angier and Alfred Borden, rival stage magicians in late 19th-century London. Both men are brilliant and ambitious. Both want to be the best. The film follows the obsessive drive of each to outperform the other in creating the most compelling, convincing stage illusion possible. But underneath their competitive ambitions lie the seeds of murder and self-destruction. Their rivalry, fueled by pride and envy, wreaks havoc in their personal and professional lives and (spoiler alert!), not everyone survives. *The Prestige* is a suspenseful and well-made film, a tragic story that illustrates why envy, the second of the seven deadly sins, made the list so many centuries ago.

In this chapter, we will see how envy is a sickness of the soul, look at the symptoms of this disease, and then learn the cure.

A Sickness of the Soul

Sin is a moral sickness of the soul. We're on good biblical grounds to think about sin in terms of a sickness or disease, for the prophets of the Old Testament and Jesus himself spoke about sin in these terms. Isaiah described God's people as a sinful nation in which "the whole head is sick, and the whole heart faint. From the sole of the foot even to the head, there is no soundness in it, but bruises and sores and raw wounds" (Isaiah 1:5b–6a). And when Jesus was criticized for attending the parties and banquets of disreputable sinners, he said, "Those who are well have no need of a physician, but those who are sick. I came not to call the righteous, but sinners" (Mark 2:17).

But while all sin can be likened to disease, this is especially true of envy. Proverbs 14:30 says, "A tranquil heart gives life to the flesh, but envy makes the bones rot." The Greek philosopher Socrates called envy "the ulcer of the soul."[41] And the fourth century church father, Basil of Caesarea, said, "No vice more pernicious than envy is implanted in the souls of men" and called envy a "disease which is gnawing at [one's] vitals and consuming them."[42] Envy, in other words, is a sickness of the soul, a consuming, wasting spiritual disease that devours its host from the inside out.

So, what is envy? Thomas Aquinas called envy "sorrow 'for another's good.'"[43] This was in keeping with Aristotle who called envy "a disturbing pain excited by the prosperity of others."[44] Jonathan Edwards said that envy is "a spirit of opposition to others' comparative happiness, or the happiness of others considered as compared with their own."[45] And here's my favorite: Frederick Buechner defines envy as "the consuming desire to have everybody else as unsuccessful as you are."[46]

Paul speaks against the impulse of envy when he tells the Romans, "Rejoice with those who rejoice, weep with those who weep" (Romans 12:15). Rejoice in the blessings that others receive, and also weep with them, showing genuine sympathy for their pain. The envious person, of course, does the opposite—rejoicing at the misfortunes of others (perhaps quietly) and growing sad when they are blessed, especially if they seem undeserving. The German word *schadenfreude* captures the heart of envy: it means "malicious joy."

In an ancient Jewish story, an angel visits a shop-keeper known for envying his rival. The angel offers to give him whatever he wishes, but warns him that his competitor will receive twice as much of whatever he asks. The shopkeeper thinks for a moment and then asks to be blind in one eye.[47]

At its core, envy is highly competitive and has an inflated sense of entitlement. The envious person thinks that all goods—whether the pleasures of life, material prosperity, or natural endowments such as brains, beauty, or opportunity—should be equally distributed to all. As essayist Joseph Epstein writes, "'Why does he have it and not I?' That is the chief, perhaps the only, question, for the envious."[48]

Dorothy Sayers calls envy the sin "which hates to see other men happy." Therefore, it seeks to level the playing field. "Envy is the great leveler: if it cannot level things up, it will level them down ... At its best, envy is a climber and a snob; at its worst it is a destroyer; rather than have anyone happier than itself, it will see us all miserable together."[49]

Examples of envy are not difficult to find. Think of the wicked queen, consumed in her quest to be the "fairest of them all" in Grimm's fairy tale "Snow White and the Seven Dwarves." Consider also the oft-cited example of

Salieri's envy of Mozart in Peter Schaeffer's play *Amadeus*. Or, if you have children, just pay attention at the breakfast table tomorrow morning: envy is the vice at work in most cases of sibling rivalry. Remember Jan Brady bemoaning her older sister's popularity in *The Brady Bunch*? "Well, all day long at school I hear how great Marcia is at this or how wonderful Marcia did that! Marcia, Marcia, Marcia!"

Perhaps the best illustration of envy in Scripture is the story of King Saul in the book of 1 Samuel. Saul was Israel's first king, but his disobedience to the Lord resulted in having the kingdom torn away from him. But even after David's secret anointing by Samuel, Saul remained the *de facto* king of Israel. The narrative of 1 Samuel depicts Saul's desperate attempt to cling to his throne at all costs. At first he is friendly to David, the young shepherd boy, whose musical talent soothes Saul's troubled spirit. But after David kills Goliath, Saul hears the women of Israel singing David's praises, "Saul has struck down his thousands, and David his ten thousands," and Saul is enraged. The text says that "Saul was very angry, and this saying displeased him. He said, 'They have ascribed to David ten thousands, and to me they have ascribed thousands, and what more can he have but the kingdom?' And Saul eyed David from that day on" (1 Samuel 18:8–9). *Saul eyed David*. The evil eye of jealous envy. And as the story continues, Saul's envy turns to suspicion, then hate, and then numerous attempts to murder David.

The Symptoms of Envy

If envy is a sickness of the soul, what are its symptoms? While envy is easy to detect when depicted in literature or on the screen, it's not always so easily discerned in our own hearts. But when we understand how envy manifests itself in other sins, we'll be better equipped to diagnose its presence in ourselves.

This was one of the reasons the church fathers compiled the list of vices in the first place. It wasn't that they considered these sins the worst of all sins, but that they viewed them as the sins from which all other sins spring. As I said earlier, they are the root sins, the principal sins, the head sins. This is also a biblical concept, for we read in James that "where you have envy and selfish ambition, there you find disorder and every evil practice" (James 3:16, NIV). So, what are the symptoms of envy?

Comparison

The first symptom of envy is comparison. Francis Bacon said, "Envy is ever joined to the comparing of a man's self; and where there is no comparison, no envy."[50] When we are envious we are always comparing ourselves with others. Have you ever felt a twinge of envy after seeing Facebook photos of some distant friend's summer vacation? Do you ever measure your education, income, house, or car in the balance with those of your siblings, neighbors, or church friends, and then harbor secret resentment towards them when you find your own life wanting? The Roman poet Horace said, "The envious man grows thin at another man's prosperity."[51]

This is exactly what we see happening in the story of Saul and David mentioned above. Saul's envy of David began with comparison. Rebecca Manley Pippert, in a fine study on David and Saul, says there are four stages of envy: 1. Making comparisons; 2. Dejection and depression; 3. A desire to harm; and 4. Irrationality.[52]

In one of his sermons, Billy Graham recounted an ancient Greek story about an athlete who was envious of one of his rivals. This rival was a celebrated champion in the games, loved and honored by the people. When they built the champion a statue, the other athlete vowed to destroy it, so deep was his hatred and envy. Every night, hidden in the cover of darkness, he chiseled away at the base of the statue to make it fall. And he succeeded, but to his own ruin, for the statue fell on him and killed him. He was a victim of his own envy.[53]

We are too often like Peter in John 21. In this story, Jesus has been raised from the dead and Peter has just been restored to fellowship with him, having thrice denied Jesus on the night of his betrayal. Jesus tells Peter that he, Peter, has yet to face the difficult trial of a painful death. And then Peter turns and looks at John, the disciple Jesus loved, and says, "Lord, what about this man?" (John 21:21) That's what comparison does. It always looks at someone else and says, "What about him? What about her?" But Jesus says to us, as he said to Peter, "What is that to you? You follow me!" (John 21:22b).

Criticizing and Complaining

The next two symptoms can be taken together: criticizing and complaining. When the envious person reflects on her own fortunes, she complains. When she reflects on the good fortunes of others, she criticizes. Of his own situation, the man consumed with envy says "It's not fair!" And of others, "They don't deserve it!"

Plantinga says that envy "is a motive that prompts people to slice up other people's reputations, to disparage their achievements, to minimize their virtues, to question their motives, to challenge their integrity . . . and, failing other ways of bringing them down, to kill them."[54]

If you sometimes find yourself criticizing people who are more educated, wealthier, or more physically attractive than yourself, you may be gripped by the vice of envy.

Ingratitude

Envy is also evident in our lack of gratitude. As one author puts it, "envy is blind to its own gifts."[55] When you're in the clutches of envy, you fail to see all the undeserved goodness that God and others have already shown to you. Are you healthy? Do you have all your faculties? Are you employed? Is there any danger of skipping a meal this week? Most of us have at least some of these blessings, and many of us presently have them all. But when we're envious, we're not thinking of what we have. We're thinking of what we don't have, especially in comparison to what someone else has.

We're like the dwarves in *The Last Battle*, who were so worried that others could have more or better food than they did, that they failed to taste the food they had, and more seriously, failed to heed the call of Aslan himself.[56] That's what envy does. It blinds us to the good we already have. And it can blind us to the God who is our ultimate good.

Hatred

Envy also leads to hatred. This was the case with Cain and Abel, when Cain's envy of Abel led to the first family feud and, tragically, the first murder.

The most vivid description of envy I am familiar

with comes from the Roman poet Ovid's narrative poem *Metamorphosis*:

> Her eyes are all awry, her teeth are foul with mould;
> green poisonous gall overflows her breast, and
> venom drips from her tongue. She never smiles, save
> at the sight of another's troubles; she never sleeps,
> disturbed with wakeful cares; unwelcome to her is
> the sight of men's success, and with the sight she pines
> away: she gnaws and is gnawed, herself her own
> punishment.[57]

What a depiction of the hatred that characterizes envy!

The Cure for Envy

Thankfully, there is a cure for souls that are sick with sin, including the sin of envy. The cure begins with recognition of the problem itself, and its origin in the pride of our sinful hearts. As Jesus said, "What comes out of a person is what defiles him. For from within, out of the heart of man, [comes] . . . envy" (Mark 7:20, 22e). And as we saw in the last chapter, pride is the taproot of all other sins.

Augustine recognized this and pointed to the humility of Christ as the remedy for envy.

> Because nothing is more contrary to love than envy,
> and the mother of envy is pride, the Lord Jesus
> Christ, the God-Man, is both the proof of God's love
> towards us, and the pattern of the humility which
> befits us men; so that the gross tumor of our sickness
> might be healed by the antidote of a medicine more

potent. Great is the wretchedness of man's pride; but greater is the mercy of God's humility.[58]

Let's think for a moment about how the Scriptures apply the potent medicine of the gospel to the tumors of our sin. To extend the analogy further, we could say there are two ways the gospel works healing for our souls. First, it functions as an emetic, purging sins such as envy from our souls. And second, the gospel feeds our hungry souls with the heart-nourishing, soul-strengthening spiritual milk of God's goodness revealed in Christ. In the words of the apostle Peter, "So put away all malice and all deceit and hypocrisy and envy and all slander. Like newborn infants, long for the pure spiritual milk, that by it you may grow up into salvation—if indeed you have tasted that the Lord is good" (1 Peter 2:1–3).

The first command in this passage is straightforward: get rid of envy (along with malice, deceit, hypocrisy, and slander). Peter's wording evokes the image of taking off an old or dirty set of clothes. It's the same idea we find in Paul's familiar "put off" and "put on" language in Ephesians 4 and Colossians 3. This is the negative aspect of the sanctification process. Theologians call it both repentance (turning from sin) and mortification (putting sin to death). Both words are important and helpful, showing us that pursuing holiness involves both changing directions and exerting holy violence against the vices that plague us.

Dealing with envy therefore involves all the disciplines of repentance: recognizing and acknowledging the sin, confessing it to the Lord, trusting his forgiveness, and taking proactive steps to replace the horde of envy-related sins (comparison, complaining, criticizing, ingratitude, and hatred) with the virtues of gratitude, contentment, and love.

But if you're like me, this is easier said than done. There is an emotional counterpart to envy that does not simply vanish on command. When I'm feeling discontent after hearing about a friend's lavish family vacation, or begin to harbor critical thoughts about a more successful pastor or author (yes, I've actually done this), I need more than a simple command to "stop it!"

But Peter's words do give us more—so much more. He tells us not only to put away envy, but also to desire something better. "Like newborn infants, long for the pure spiritual milk, that by it you may grow up into salvation—if indeed you have tasted that the Lord is good." The most effective medicine for envy is the pure spiritual milk of God's goodness. And as the following verses show, God's goodness is supremely revealed in Christ, who as "a living stone rejected by men but in the sight of God chosen and precious" (1 Peter 2:4), embraced the humiliation of the cross and is now exalted as the head of the church, the cornerstone of the new "spiritual house" of living stones (v 5).

Christ shows us both the goodness of God's love and the pattern of self-giving humility that seeks the good of others. Love and humility are embodied in Jesus. This is the medicine that heals our envious hearts.

Jonathan Edwards understood this. So when he wanted to help his people fight envy, he didn't just exhort them to stop envying one another, but skillfully applied the gospel to their hearts.

The doctrines of the gospel teach us how far Jesus Christ was from grudging us anything which he could do for or give to us. He did not grudge us a life spent in labor and suffering; he did not grudge us his own precious blood; he hath not grudged us a sitting with him on his throne in heaven, and being partakers with him of that heavenly kingdom and glory which the Father hath given him . . . The Christian scheme of doctrine teaches us how Christ came into the world to deliver us from the fruits of Satan's envy towards us. The devil being miserable himself envied mankind that happiness which they had, and could not bear to see our first parents in their happy state in Eden, and therefore exerted himself to the utmost to ruin them, and accomplished it. The gospel teaches how Christ came into the world to destroy the works of the devil, and deliver us from that misery into which his envy had brought us.[59]

The gospel is the medicine that cures bone-rotting envy. It's the radiation that kills this cancer of malicious joy. And it's "the expulsive power of a new affection,"[60] the taste of something better, that delivers us from the chocolate-covered, yet poisonous morsels of comparing, criticizing, complaining, ingratitude, and hatred.

Examine and Apply

1. Check yourself for the symptoms of envy: are you given to comparison, criticism, and complaining? Is your life characterized by ingratitude?
2. Have you nurtured a secret hatred in your heart for

people more successful, beautiful, or prosperous than you?

3. Think about this: the Lord Jesus Christ is the least envious person in the entire universe! Read Philippians 2:5–11 and consider his complete lack of pride, envy, and jealousy, then meditate on his humble self-giving love, asking the Spirit to remove the envy in your heart.

Four
WRATH

One of the dumbest fights I've ever had with my wife, Holly, was over a movie. I had been waiting months for a new blockbuster film to hit the theaters, so as soon as it was out we settled on a plan and I purchased an advance ticket. (Yes, this was a solo operation.) The day finally arrived, and I was primed for a great experience.

But guess what? Some friends invited us over for a cookout that very evening, and Holly really wanted to go. Immediately I began to struggle in my heart—*but... my movie...this wasn't the plan!* When Holly pressed the issue a little further, I erupted like a volcano. In retrospect it seems ridiculous, but a molten rage inside my heart had reached the boiling point, and out of my mouth spewed a stream of words hot as lava.

Holly responded with great grace and clarity, calmly pointing out that my desire to see this movie had obviously become *way* too important to me. In fact, as she indicated, it had become an idol.

I'd like to report that I immediately saw the error of my ways and repented. But I didn't. We did, however, come up with a compromise—I attended a matinee and we went to the cookout that night, both of us wearing forced smiles.

Two other facts that make this story even more embarrassing for me. First, Holly had delivered our third child about six weeks before and desperately needed some social interaction. Second, the movie I had made an idol of in this kerfuffle wasn't a thoughtful art film or an Oscar-worthy biopic of a noted historical figure. It was *Spiderman 3*, which even filmmaker Sam Raimi's most ardent fans admit was clearly the low point in that trilogy.

And here's the twist: *Spiderman 3* was the installment where Peter Parker becomes a total jerk. After being contaminated by an extraterrestrial symbiote that exacerbates his worst tendencies, transforming him into a black-suited Spiderman hell-bent on selfishness and revenge, he completely blows it with both Gwen Stacy and Mary Jane. As bad as the film was, the themes of anger and forgiveness were integral to the plot. These ironies were not lost on me as I sat there in the theater that afternoon, feeling conviction for my nasty attitude and angry words to Holly. Unlike Peter Parker, though, I had no symbiote to blame. Only myself.

The Diagnosis of Wrath

My sinful anger in this story is obvious. But diagnosing wrath isn't always easy, nor its danger always apparent. If we want to deal with wrath biblically, we need both an accurate diagnosis and a realistic prognosis.

Sinful Wrath vs. Righteous Anger

One reason anger is difficult to diagnose is that it's not always sinful. Although rare, there actually is such a thing as righteous indignation. In Ephesians 4:26 we read, "Be angry and do not sin; do not let the sun go down on your anger." Quoting from Psalm 4, Paul concedes that we will sometimes be angry. While warning us not to sin in our anger or let the sun set with wrath still in our hearts, he nevertheless doesn't condemn anger categorically.

Even the Lord Jesus experienced (holy) anger. Early in his ministry, the scrupulous Pharisees—with granite-hard hearts and eyes more critical than those of an Olympic judge—watched to see whether Jesus would heal on the Sabbath. And Jesus "looked around at them *with anger*, grieved at their hardness of heart, and said to the man, 'Stretch out your hand.' He stretched it out, and his hand was restored" (Mark 3:5).

Aristotle praised the person "who gets angry at the right things and with the right people, and also in the right way and at the right time and for the right length of time."[61] The word Aristotle used to describe this kind of person is the same word found in Scripture for *meekness* or *gentleness*. A meek or a gentle person is a person whose anger is rightly ordered: directed at the right things and expressed in an appropriate manner. Wrath, on the other hand, is the "love of justice perverted to revenge and spite."[62]

Rightly ordered anger is in fact an important and necessary component of true love. Sometimes it is *right* to be angry. When wicked people prey upon the weak and helpless, love for the victims demands anger and the pursuit of justice.

C. S. Lewis once said, "anger is the fluid that love bleeds when you cut it."[63] That's why we innately feel anger when someone threatens the well-being of our children. Such anger must be free from malice to be sure, but this doesn't mean the anger itself should be suppressed. Jesus didn't mildly suggest that the moneychangers in the temple ply their trade elsewhere. He turned over their tables and drove them out with a whip! We *should* be angry at child abuse, domestic violence, abortion, sex trafficking, school shootings, racism, and more. The lack of anger at such evil suggests indifference and the failure of love.

Several years ago, I was legitimately and deeply angry when a close friend and member of our church abandoned his family, divorced his wife, and married the woman with whom he had committed adultery. He had broken his vows and the hearts of those who loved him. My anger was mingled with tears and a genuine longing for his repentance. But it was still anger.

So how can you distinguish the sin of wrath from righteous anger? Robert Jones offers three criteria:

1. Righteous anger reacts against actual sin.
2. Righteous anger focuses on God and his kingdom, rights, and concerns, not on me and my kingdom, rights, and concerns.
3. Righteous anger is accompanied by other godly qualities and expresses itself in godly ways.[64]

Even with these criteria, getting an accurate read on your anger requires the heart-searching ministry of the Holy Spirit, and sometimes the insight of a discerning counselor or pastor with well-developed skills in soul care.

But of this you can be sure: if you foam with frantic fury when your three year old spills her milk *again*, or if you simmer silently in seething resentment because someone cut you off in traffic, or if (hypothetically) you detonate in an explosive outburst of rage over not getting to see a movie, your wrath is sinful.

The Complexity of Anger

Proverbs tells us that the ways of a person given to anger are a snare (Proverbs 22:24–25). And like any effective snare, anger is carefully camouflaged. Anger is psychologically complex, involving our minds, hearts, and wills. "Anger is more than mere emotion, volition, cognition or behavior … Anger is complex. It comprises the whole person and encompasses our whole package of beliefs, feelings, actions, and desires."[65]

That's a vital point: *the whole person is involved in anger*—not just our emotions, but our thoughts, beliefs, actions, and desires. We should therefore be careful not to think of the sin of anger just in terms of one set of emotions and responses. Just as the initial symptoms of a disease can vary greatly from one person to another, so the vice of wrath can show up in various ways. You may not have a short fuse, but that doesn't mean you're free from wrath.

Knowing that anger involves the whole person also explains why wrath, of all the capital sins, may be the most difficult to acknowledge *as sin*. We're miserable in envy, depressed by sloth, and embarrassed by gluttony and lust. Those sins may be hard to admit to others, but not usually to ourselves. Wrath is different. We can be deeply angry without fully realizing we're sinning because *anger usually feels so right*. Wrath is a chameleon adept at disguise, quickly adapting its color to a variety of background reasons and rationalizations.

Sinful Anger as a Violation of Love

One of the best ways to detect sinful anger is by setting it in contrast to love. . As we saw above, there is a kind of anger that is fully compatible with love. But when wrath overruns love, we're in trouble. In the Bible's most heart-probing description of love, Paul tells us that love "is not irritable or resentful" (1 Corinthians 13:5b). The language Paul uses is much more vivid and evocative than English translations usually convey. As Anthony Thiselton notes, Paul uses "dynamic pictorial imagery in which every verb depicts an action or stance, usually under the guise of a metaphor or pictorial image." "Irritable" conveys the image of "being probed with a sharp spike," while "resentful" pictures "an accountant reckoning up accounts."[66] These pictures show us the two primary ways that sinful anger violates love.

Hot anger. To be irritable is *to get angry too easily*. This is hot anger: the easily provoked, quick-tempered wrath of a volatile hothead who flies into fits of rage at the slightest aggravation. Proverbs shows us that this kind of anger is hasty, foolish, and given to stirring up strife. "Whoever is slow to anger has great understanding, but he who has a hasty temper exalts folly" (Proverbs 14:29). "A hot-tempered man stirs up strife, but he who is slow to anger quiets contention" (Proverbs 15:18).

Cold anger. To be resentful, on the other hand, is *to stay angry for too long*. This is cold anger: the record-keeping wrath of a bitter, cold-hearted person who always remembers, never forgets, and never forgives.

One counselor calls these two kinds of anger *ventilation* and *internalization*, *blowing up* and *clamming up*.[67] Most of us are more given to one form than the other. Some people shout, others pout. But whether you spew or stew, the underlying anger in either case is a violation of love. And either violation is sinful and dangerous.

The Root Cause of Anger Is Idolatrous Desire

So far we've only dealt with symptoms, but good diagnosis goes further and discerns causes. And in Scripture, the basic root cause of anger is *desire*. We see this in James 4:1–2: "What causes quarrels and what causes fights among you? Is it not this, that your passions are at war within you? You desire and do not have, so you murder. You covet and cannot obtain, so you fight and quarrel."

James is telling us that *warring desires* are behind every quarrel and fight, whether the expression of anger is hot or cold. The word he uses for *desire* is an important and vivid word: *epithumeo*. It means not just a desire, but a deep desire, a desire in overdrive, an inordinate desire. It's the verbal form of the word James uses in James 1:14–15: "But each person is tempted when he is lured and enticed by his own *desire* (*epithumia*). Then *desire* when it has conceived gives birth to sin, and sin when it is fully grown brings forth death."

The old theological word for this kind of desire is *concupiscence*. While we normally associate concupiscence with inordinate sexual desire, the biblical concept includes any and all desires that lead us into sin. "For James, concupiscence is our fallen inclination to sin, such that our own corrupt hearts and wills are the authors of sin and it is they we must blame and not God. Concupiscence (original sin) conceives actual sin and actual sin brings death."[68]

Sinful wrath is the offspring of inordinate, idolatrous desire. It may be a desire for justice, esteem, comfort, approval, or security. None of these desires are wrong in and of themselves. But when we seek the fulfillment of these desires in ways that violate God's will, our desires have become inordinate. And when someone crosses our inordinate desires? Watch out! What follows may be a hot torrent of molten anger or the slow onslaught of an icy glacier of resentment. But one way or the other, idolatrous hearts are spring-loaded to retaliate once their desires are crossed.

The Prognosis for Wrath

But why is wrath dangerous? Is losing my temper really that big of a deal? Are the consequences of misman-aged anger really that severe? The answer of Scripture is *yes*. Sinful anger is both serious and dangerous for several reasons. It dishonors God (James 1:19–20), hurts relationships (Proverbs 29:22), gives Satan an advantage (Ephesians 4:26–27), hinders prayer (1 Timothy 2:8), and apart from grace, will keep you out of God's kingdom (Galatians 5:19–21).

In short, wrath is dangerous because it's a capital sin. Capital sins, as we've already seen, are leading sins, gateway sins. Vices, like military captains, bring hordes of other sins with them. And this is particularly true of wrath. As Gregory said, "From anger are produced strifes, swelling of mind, insults, clamour, indignation, blasphemies."[69] The sin of wrath spoils friendships, splits churches, shatters business partnerships, fractures marriages, alienates children and parents, and estranges our hearts from God. How many homes and churches are spiritual and emotional Chernobyls, devastated by the radioactive fallout of sinful wrath?

As a pastor, I've seen the long-term devastation of harbored anger up close and personal. One of my saddest experiences was standing in a hospital room at the bed of a woman from our church. She was dying and knew it. But still she refused any attempt at reconciliation with her estranged children. She was so bitter from the hurts of years gone by that she wouldn't even let them come see her. I prayed with her. I read to her Jesus' sobering words, "If you forgive others their trespasses, your heavenly Father will also forgive you, but if you do not forgive others their trespasses, neither will your Father forgive your trespasses" (Matthew 6:14–15). But she would not budge. There was no way she would extend forgiveness to her children.

One of saddest things about anger is that *it destroys you*. In the words of Frederick Buechner:

> Of the Seven Deadly Sins, anger is possibly the most fun. To lick your wounds, to smack your lips over grievances long past, to roll over your tongue the prospect of bitter confrontations still to come, to savor to the last toothsome morsel both the pain you are given and the pain you are giving back—in many ways it is a feast fit for a king. The chief drawback is that what you are wolfing down is yourself. The skeleton at the feast is you.[70]

Jesus was no less serious in his warning. In the Sermon on the Mount, he said,

> You have heard that it was said to those of old, "You shall not murder; and whoever murders will be liable to judgment." But I say to you that everyone who is angry with his brother will be liable to judgment; whoever insults his brother will be liable to the

council; and whoever says, "You fool!" will be liable to the hell of fire (Matthew 5:21–22).

Why such a stern warning? Not just because anger breaks God's law and deserves his judgment, though that of course is true; but also because vented anger and harbored resentment harden our hearts, shrivel our spirits, and shrink our souls, leaving us distorted and malformed by sin. As Anne Lamott said, "Not forgiving is like drinking rat poison and then waiting for the rat to die."[71] For sin not only makes you guilty, it changes you in the deepest core of your being.

Even when the outward effects of sinful anger are not as severe, the distortion and pollution caused in our inner being is very real. As Lewis wrote,

> One man may be so placed that his anger sheds the blood of thousands, and another so placed that however angry he gets he will only be laughed at. But the little mark on the soul may be much the same in both. Each has done something to himself which, unless he repents, will make it harder for him to keep out of the rage next time he is tempted, and will make the rage worse when he does fall into it. Each of them, if he seriously turns to God, can have that twist in the central man straightened out again: each is, in the long run, doomed if he will not. The bigness or smallness of the thing, seen from the outside, is not what really matters.[72]

The Remedy for Wrath

How then do we "seriously turn to God" to "have that twist in the central man straightened out again"? How does the gospel equip us to deal with the sin of wrath? What is the remedy for anger? There are three basic ingredients to this remedy.

Identify the Idols

First, you need to discern the underlying idolatry of your heart. What are you angry about? What deep desire has been thwarted? What personal right (whether real or perceived) has been violated? *How have your desires been crossed?*

Let's go back to my anger over the movie. What was the idol behind my outburst of wrath? I think there was a cluster of idols: the desire for entertainment, my perception of my "right" to stick to a plan we had agreed on beforehand, and (clearly) the elevation of my own wishes above the well-being of Holly or the way of Jesus. The occasion of the anger wasn't really the issue. A movie is a silly reason to get in a fight. But the occasion revealed something about my heart. It revealed a heart that, at that moment, was resting not in Jesus, but in the fulfillment of self-centered desires.

When the underlying idols of our hearts are complex and difficult to discern—which is often the case with anger—we can frequently get diagnostic hints by looking at our anger patterns. Here, I suggest you chronicle your anger in a journal. Take a month and write down every time you lose your temper, or say something harsh or hurtful to others, or find yourself harboring bitterness. Briefly describe the circumstances, the apparent trigger that "set you off," and your response. When the month is finished, prayerfully look for patterns. Ask the Lord to show you the root system of idolatrous desires underlying your angry behavior.

Refrain from Anger and Forsake Wrath

The second ingredient is repentance. In the words of Psalm 37:8: "Refrain from anger, and forsake wrath! Fret not yourself; it tends only to evil." Repentance involves both confessing and forsaking sin, and will often involve making restitution or seeking reconciliation with another person. After warning about the danger of anger, Jesus said, "So if you are offering your gift at the altar and there remember that your brother has something against you, leave your gift there before the altar and go. First be reconciled to your brother, and then come and offer your gift" (Matthew 5:23–24). Reconciliation may not always be possible, but we are responsible to open ourselves to it by confessing our wrath and seeking forgiveness.

None of this is to imply that our repentance will ever be perfect or can in any way merit forgiveness. Repentance is just the reverse side of faith. Turning to the Lord means taking his side against our sins and setting our hearts on obedience once again. True faith is repentant faith. Yet the assurance of our pardon rests not in the quality of our repentance, but in the fullness of God's grace given to us in Christ. Repentance isn't about trying to get our act together so that God will forgive us. To use the words of John Piper, repentance is not a "job description" but a "doctor's prescription."[73] When we trust our physician, we will embrace his prescribed regimen for renewed health.

Embrace a Life of Forgiveness

The third ingredient sweetens the others: embrace a life of forgiveness. By this I mean not only that we should embrace the call to forgive others, but embrace also the forgiveness God freely offers to all who trust in Jesus.

When Jesus taught his disciples to pray, he said:

Pray then like this: "Our Father in heaven, hallowed be your name. Your kingdom come, your will be done, on earth as it is in heaven. Give us this day our daily bread, and forgive us our debts, as we also have forgiven our debtors. And lead us not into temptation, but deliver us from evil. For if you forgive others their trespasses, your heavenly Father will also forgive you, but if you do not forgive others their trespasses, neither will your Father forgive your trespasses" (Matthew 6:9–15).

Jesus was not laying down a mechanical condition for being forgiven by God. He was showing us that when the dynamic power of God's grace is working in our hearts, it leads us into a life characterized by forgiveness. When we really taste the sweetness of God's free grace and bask in the light of his forgiveness, the deepest impulse of our hearts will be to extend that same grace and forgiveness to others.

Earlier in this chapter, we saw that the sin of wrath is a violation of love. But Jesus perfectly personified love, thus showing us the heart of God. And remember, "love is not irritable or resentful" (1 Corinthians 13:5b). This means God is not easily irritated! The Bible tells us repeatedly that God is "slow to anger." He is not the least bit prone to temper tantrums. "The LORD is merciful and gracious, slow to anger and abounding in steadfast love" (Psalm 103:8).

Nor is God resentful. He doesn't keep a record of our wrongs (2 Corinthians 5:18–19). If you are in Christ, my friend, you can rest assured that God is not keeping a tally chart of your sins. He doesn't count our trespasses against us. He has "forgiven us all our trespasses, by canceling the record of debt that stood against us with its legal demands. This he set aside, nailing it to the cross" (Colossians 2:13c–14). In the wonderful words of Horatio Spafford:

> *My sin, O the bliss of this glorious thought!*
> *My sin, not in part, but the whole*
> *Is nailed to the cross, and I bear it no more*
> *Praise the Lord, praise the Lord, O my soul.*[74]

God's love and forgiveness are powerful enough to quench the flames of your hot temper or melt the glacier of your cold and bitter heart. Embracing a life of forgiveness means embracing God's forgiveness and allowing the power of his grace to transform you so that you gradually become an ever more merciful and forgiving person.

Examine and Apply

1. Does your anger run hot or cold? Are you more prone to blowing up or clamming up? If you're married, discuss this with your spouse. It's not unusual for spouses to be opposites in this area.
2. What are the idols driving your anger and resentment? If you're not sure, try keeping a journal where you honestly write down *why* you feel angry or resentful.
3. Do you need to reconcile a broken relationship?
4. Have you embraced the forgiveness God offers to you in Christ? Is your heart captivated by the depth of his mercy and the freedom of his grace?

Five
SLOTH

Of the seven capital sins, sloth may be the least understood. Most of us probably associate it either with TV-addled couch potatoes or those odd, tree-dwelling mammals that TV-addled couch potatoes watch on the Nature Channel. If we associate *sloth* with sin at all, we likely think of the sluggard described in the book of Proverbs. In short, we tend to equate it with physical laziness. Laziness is a problem, of course, and may be a symptom of sloth. But even busy, hard-working people can be stuck in this vice.

The deadly-sin type of sloth is actually more sinister than laziness. Dorothy Sayers said,

> [It] is insidious, and assumes such Protean shapes that it is rather difficult to define. It is not merely idleness of mind and laziness of body: it is that whole poisoning of the will which, beginning with indifference and an attitude of "I couldn't care less," extends to the deliberate refusal of joy and culminates in morbid introspection and despair.[75]

If there's one sin besides pride that is a seedbed for all

the others, it is sloth. Sloth is "the accomplice of the other sins and their worst punishment."[76] As a medieval moral tract called *Jacob's Well* put it, "when the devil finds a slothful person, empty and void of good works, he sends the other sins to dwell within him."[77]

So, what is the sin of sloth, why is it dangerous, and what can we do to overcome it?

What is Sloth?

In the history of Christian spirituality, sloth has two components: *acedia* (apathy) and *tristitia* (sadness). *Acedia*, meaning "without care," implies "an aimless indifference to one's responsibilities to God and to man."[78] Sayers called this, "the sin that believes in nothing, cares for nothing, seeks to know nothing, interferes with nothing, enjoys nothing, loves nothing, hates nothing, finds purpose in nothing, lives for nothing, and remains alive only because there is nothing it would die for."[79]

Tristitia, on the other hand, means sorrow or sadness and suggests spiritual depression or despair. The two sins were originally separate on the list, but eventually coalesced into the single vice of sloth. R. R. Reno, combining the two ideas, calls this sin "a lassitude and despair that overwhelms spiritual striving."[80]

The biblical passage that has best helped me understand sloth is Hebrews 5:11–6:12. This section is an *inclusio*: a literary device in which a word or phrase bookends the beginning and end of a passage, forming a frame. This is a well-known technique in ancient writings by which authors helped their readers focus on the main point.

The beginning of this particular frame reads, "On this topic we have much to say and it is difficult to explain, since you have become *sluggish* ['dull,' ESV] in hearing" (Hebrews 5:11, NET). The end of the frame reads, "But we passionately want each of you to demonstrate the same eagerness for the fulfillment of your hope until the end, so that you may not be *sluggish* ['slothful,' KJV], but imitators of those who through faith and perseverance inherit the promises" (Hebrews 6:11–12, NET).

The key word here is *sluggish*. The Greek word basically means lazy or slothful. Its use in 5:11 shows the kind slothfulness or sluggishness the writer has in mind, "sluggish in hearing." The author is exhorting his audience to hear the gospel, the word God has spoken by his Son. But they have grown lazy in their hearing. "Their difficulty is not simply mental laziness but spiritual resistance. They are now unwilling to work out the deeper implications of the gospel in their lives."[81]

That phrase "spiritual resistance" perfectly captures the essence of sloth. Rebecca DeYoung calls sloth "resistance to the demands of love."[82] In Dante, we encounter *acedia* (apathy) in those who suffer from, "a slow love that cannot motivate and uplift, leaving the soul stagnant, unable to move under the heavy burden of sin."[83]

In his classic work on indwelling sin, John Owen uncovered four features of spiritual sloth in this passage from Hebrews. To paraphrase him, sloth is characterized by carelessness, unwillingness to act, half-hearted effort, and becoming easily discouraged by any possible difficulty.[84]

Carelessness

This is what Owen calls "inadvertency." Essentially, it means negligence. One of the sluggard passages in Proverbs provides the perfect example:

I passed by the field of a sluggard, by the vineyard of a man lacking sense, and behold, it was all overgrown with thorns; the ground was covered with nettles, and its stone wall was broken down. Then I saw and considered it; I looked and received instruction. A little sleep, a little slumber, a little folding of the hands to rest, and poverty will come upon you like a robber, and want like an armed man. (Proverbs 24:30–34)

The lesson is that neglect leads to poverty. Carelessness and neglect also have dire consequences in the spiritual life.

Unwillingness to Act

This is procrastination, sloth's "unwillingness to be stirred up unto its duty." "The sluggard does not plow in the autumn; he will seek at harvest and have nothing" (Proverbs 20:4). Spiritually speaking, Owen says that "there is an unwillingness in sloth to take any notice of warnings, calls, excitations, or stirrings up by the word, Spirit, judgments—anything that God makes use of to call the mind unto a due consideration of the condition of the soul."

Half-Hearted Effort

On the other hand, sometimes sloth will put on a different face and give "weak and ineffectual attempts to recover itself unto its duty." Owen compares this to the sluggard in Proverbs 26:14 ("As a door turns on its hinges, so does a sluggard on his bed") and says,

In the turning of a door upon its hinges, there is some motion but no progress . . . There where he was one

the lazy farmer who wouldn't hoe corn

day, there he is the next; yea, there where he was one year, he is the next. His endeavors are faint [and] cold … he gets no ground by them, but is always beginning and never finishing his work.

4. Discouragement in the Face of Every Difficulty

Lastly, sloth is easily discouraged so that "every difficulty deters him from duty." In fact, any excuse will suffice to keep the sluggard from his responsibilities, even an imaginary danger. "The sluggard says, 'There is a lion outside! I shall be killed in the streets!'" (Proverbs 22:13).

Why is Sloth So Dangerous?

As with all the capital sins, sloth is dangerous because it is a gateway to other sins. Gregory treated this sin under the rubric of "melancholy" and said, "From melancholy there arise malice, rancour, cowardice, despair, slothfulness in fulfilling the commands, and a wandering of the mind on unlawful objects."[85]

But sloth is somewhat unique. While it leads to other sins, it often does so indirectly. Sloth leads into patterns of thought and behavior that produce hospitable conditions for other sins to grow. As an untilled field lying fallow becomes a seedbed for a wild crop of weeds, so a slothful heart becomes fertile ground for vice.

Sloth does this in several ways.

Sloth Stunts Your Growth

We see this in Hebrews 5 in two vivid illustrations that further describe those who are dull of hearing. First, they are like scholars who should be able to instruct others, but need to learn the alphabet all over again. "For though by this time you ought to be teachers, you need someone to teach you again the basic principles of the oracles of God" (v 12a).

Second, they are like adults still needing to be bottle-fed when they should be eating table food. "You need milk, not solid food, for everyone who lives on milk is unskilled in the word of righteousness, since he is a child. But solid food is for the mature, for those who have their powers of discernment trained by constant practice to distinguish good from evil" (v 12b–14). These are pictures of spiritual retardation, prolonged immaturity, or stunted growth caused by inattentiveness to God's Word. In contrast, the next verse urges these spiritual sloths to "leave the elementary doctrine of Christ and go on to maturity" (Hebrews 6:1).

Sloth Tempts You to Quit

The second effect of sloth, even more frightening, is described in the often misunderstood words of Hebrews 6:4–6. This is the heart of the *inclusio* framed by the passages about sluggishness, and presents the main point of that section.

> For it is impossible, in the case of those who have once been enlightened, who have tasted the heavenly gift, and have shared in the Holy Spirit, and have tasted the goodness of the word of God and the powers of the age to come, and then have fallen away, to restore them again to repentance, since they are crucifying once again the Son of God to their own harm and holding him up to contempt. For land that

has drunk the rain that often falls on it, and produces a crop useful to those for whose sake it is cultivated, receives a blessing from God. But if it bears thorns and thistles, it is worthless and near to being cursed, and its end is to be burned.

There are three common interpretations of this passage.

1. A truly regenerate believer can apostatize from faith in Jesus Christ and be lost after all.
2. The list of experiences appearing in these verses are not actual evidences of salvation, but describe people who appreciate and enjoy certain aspects of Christian culture and practice but have not been converted.
3. The passage is hypothetical in nature, showing us what *would* happen if a true Christian *could* fall away from Christ.

The first interpretation I reject, because I believe Scripture teaches the eternal security of the person who has been justified by faith and indwelt by the Spirit (e.g., John 10:27–29; Romans 8:1, 33–34).[86] This doesn't mean everyone who makes a *profession* of faith will be saved. There is such a thing as temporary faith or false faith. As the old Bible teacher J. Vernon McGee used to say, "I believe in the security of the believer, and in the insecurity of the make-believer."[87]

Furthermore, we miss the thrust of this text if we apply the warning *only* to those who have made false professions of faith (that is, interpretation number two).

Therefore, we should also view the text as a warning to believers (interpretation number three) about what would happen if sloth were *allowed* to take its course in our lives. But the wonderful truth is that God will never give up on the sanctification of his children, however far they may fall into sin. If he has begun a good work in us, he will be faithful to complete it (Philippians 1:6). Nevertheless, this *does not negate the warning*. The promises assure us of God's preserving grace, while this and other warnings in Scripture serve as one of God's means for *keeping us* in that grace.

So, sloth is clearly dangerous because it stunts our growth in Christ—so much so, in fact, that were it not for God's preserving and sanctifying grace, it could actually cause us to quit and thus fall away from faith in Christ. Make no mistake; sloth can do real and serious harm to your faith.

Sloth Never Leaves You in Neutral

Hebrews 6:4–6 also shows us that spiritual sloth never leaves us in neutral. If you're not moving forward, you will drift backwards. You will either grow or decay. There is no standing still. The spiritual life is not like riding a bike, where you learn once and never forget. It's more like golf: neglect your short game for a few weeks, and you'll be chipping over the green and triple-putting.

Sloth Takes Advantage of the Middle Period

Finally, be wary of particular situations where the temptation to sloth is strongest. Martyn Lloyd-Jones called this the difficulty of the "middle period."[88]

Lloyd-Jones, who was also medically trained, had unique diagnostic skills as a pastor, making him a superb physician of souls. In *Spiritual Depression*, Lloyd-Jones discussed spiritual weariness in a chapter on Galatians 6:9, "And let us not be weary in well doing: for in due season we shall reap, if we faint not."

He observed that during young adulthood or when beginning something new (education, marriage, career, etc.) there is typically a honeymoon stage. Everything feels new, fresh, and exciting as you make new discoveries and enjoy new experiences for the first time. But eventually the honeymoon is over. The thrill fades and you reach the challenging part. You have to study hard to get the degree. You can't rely on romantic feelings in the marriage, but have to learn to give up selfishness and love another person. The career that at first felt like a true vocation starts to feel like a job, and you have to go to work whether you want to or not.

The same is true in the spiritual life. When you first become a Christian, there are lots of positive emotions: the joy of knowing your sins are forgiven, the thrill of learning new things from Scripture, the sense of God's presence in your life, the amazement when God first answers prayer in a tangible way, the excitement of someone responding when you share your faith.

But dry periods invariably come. The glow of the spiritual honeymoon fades away, you learn that faith doesn't make you immune to suffering, and many prayers seem to go unanswered. It's during this season that the temptation to sloth becomes especially strong.

You might be there now. Maybe you're wrestling through a mid-life crisis. Perhaps you're hitting a wall in marriage or parenting. Maybe you're halfway through graduate school and struggling to find the energy to finish.

Or it's possible you're in a spiritual desert and God feels a million miles away.

If this describes you, there is hope. Spiritual sloth *can* be resisted!

How Do You Overcome Sloth?

I want to give five answers to this question. The first three (from Lloyd-Jones) are negative; the last two are positive.

Don't Quit

One great temptation of sloth is simply to quit. But this is one thing you must not do. Don't listen to the voices in your head saying, "This is too much for me, I'm too tired to go on, I'm throwing in the towel." Those thoughts are not from God. Don't quit on marriage. Don't quit on parenting. Don't quit on Christianity. Don't quit on life.

Don't Resign Yourself to This Condition

Lloyd-Jones says the greatest temptation isn't so much to quit, but to resign yourself to your condition. All the temptations that sloth presents us with, including plain old resignation, are flat-out denials of the truth of Scripture and of God's sovereign, faithful goodness in your life. To yield to them is to call God a liar and his Word unreliable. Never let sloth tempt you to start believing that change is impossible. Never let it persuade you to let go of your hope, to go on merely in what Lloyd-Jones calls a "hopeless, dragging condition."

Don't Resort to Artificial Stimulants

One element of sloth, remember, is *tristitia*—sadness, sorrow, despair. Spiritual depression. But when we're struggling with depressed emotions, one of the temptations is to take something or do something that will give us an artificial "lift."

Some of the more obvious ways people attempt to escape involve drugs or excessive use of alcohol. But for every Christian who turns to these substances, there are dozens more who seek a high by raiding the refrigerator, vegging out on TV, or indulging in "retail therapy." As DeYoung says, "*Acedia's* greatest temptations are escapism and despair."[89]

There is a place, of course, for the medical treatment of depression; I don't doubt that physiological factors can contribute to these kinds of conditions. If you struggle with ongoing depression, I encourage you to seek professional help from both a counselor and a physician. Depression requires treatment, and we must resist the temptation of masking it or seeking an escape.

Be Earnest in Your Pursuit of Assurance

This is the exhortation in Hebrews 6:9–11. It's an encouraging passage that stands in stark relief against the warnings of verses 4–8. First, the author tells his readers that he is assured of better things concerning them, pointing out as evidence of their salvation their love for God's name and their service to the saints. But these evidences don't give them reason to coast. Instead, he tells them to "show the same earnestness to have the full assurance of hope until the end."

Assurance, you see, isn't like a birth certificate. It's not something you get, file away, and only pull out when you need to prove your identity. It's something to be pursued with diligence. In John Owen's wise words:

Are you in depths and doubts, staggering and uncertain, not knowing what is your condition, nor whether you have any interest in the forgiveness that is of God? Are you tossed up and down between hopes and fears? [Do you] want peace, consolation and establishment? Why lie you upon your faces? Get up, watch, pray, fast, meditate, offer violence to your lusts and corruptions; fear not, startle not at their crying . . . to be spared; press unto the throne of grace by prayer, supplications, importunities, restless requests. This is the way to take the kingdom of heaven. These things are not peace, they are not assurance; but they are part of the means that God hath appointed for the attainment of them.[90]

Look to the Promises of God with Persevering Faith

"And we desire each one of you to show the same earnestness to have the full assurance of hope until the end, so that you may not be sluggish, but imitators of those who through faith and patience inherit the promises" (Hebrews 6:11–12). Don't be sluggish, but imitate those who inherit the promises. But how do they inherit? "Through faith and patience" or "perseverance" (NET).

There's a scene in Bunyan's *Pilgrim's Progress* where Christian suffers a temporary defeat by the sin of sloth, during his ascent of Hill Difficulty. The hill was so steep that he "fell from running to going, and from going to clambering upon his hands and his knees." But halfway up, the pilgrim finds a pleasant arbor "made by the Lord of the hill for the refreshing of weary travelers." He stops to rest. He reads the scroll he carried in his bosom representing "the assurance of his life and acceptance at the desired haven." But in his rest, he fell into "a slumber and thence into a fast sleep, which detained him in that place until it was almost night." In sleep, the scroll slips from his hand.

Christian is awakened from his sleep with the words of Proverbs 6:6: "Go to the ant, thou sluggard; consider her ways, and be wise." He resumes his journey and climbs to the top of the hill. But on the summit he encounters Timorous and Mistrust, who are walking in the opposite direction. "Sirs, what's the matter?" Christian asks. "You run the wrong way."

"The further we go, the more danger we meet with," Timorous replies. Mistrust expresses his fear of lions on the road ahead.

Christian has met a stark choice. Will he face the difficulties and dangers ahead, or turn back in fear and unbelief? "You make me afraid, but whither shall I fly to be safe?" he says.

> If I go back to mine own country, *that* is prepared for fire and brimstone, and I shall certainly perish there. If I can get to the Celestial City, I am sure to be in safety there. I must venture. To go back is nothing but death; to go forward is fear of death, and life everlasting beyond it. I will yet go forward.

Knowing he cannot turn back, Christian continues his journey, his heart now full of doubts and fears. But when he looks for his scroll, he can't find it. He has lost his assurance. "Then was Christian in great distress, and knew not what to do." But then he remembers his sleep in the arbor so he falls upon his knees, seeks God's forgiveness, and goes back to look for his scroll. "But all the way he went back, who can sufficiently set forth the sorrow of Christian's heart? Sometimes he sighed, sometimes he wept, and oftentimes he [chided] himself for being so foolish to fall asleep in that place, which was erected only for a little refreshment from his weariness."

Christian eventually finds his scroll, grabs it "with trembling and haste," and hides it in his heart once again, giving thanks to God "for directing his eye to the place where it lay." With joyful tears, he resumes his journey.[91]

Bunyan's insight shows how easily we can be ensnared by sloth. We all face the Hill Difficulty in our journey, and we're often tempted to quit precisely in those moments when vigilance and renewed zeal are most needful. If sloth has stunted your growth or tempted you to quit, Bunyan's story shows how to recover: Repent of spiritual lethargy, embrace once again the promises of God, regain your assurance, and press on in your pilgrimage with persevering faith.

Examine and Apply

1. Do you ever struggle with apathy? You might not consider yourself a slothful person, but have you encountered spiritual resistance?

2. Think about Owen's characteristics of spiritual sloth: carelessness, unwillingness to act, half-hearted effort, and becoming easily discouraged by any possible difficulty. Are these symptoms true of you?

3. Have you faced "the difficulty of the middle period"? Are you tempted to quit or to coast?

4. How do the warnings and promises of Scripture help us to resist sloth and persevere in faith?

Six
GREED

One of my favorite classic films is John Huston's 1948 masterpiece, *The Treasure of the Sierra Madre.* Set in Mexico, it's a gripping tale of two down-and-out Americans in Tampico who meet Howard, a veteran gold prospector who takes them into the mountains of Sierra Madre to search for gold.

The film is a fascinating portrayal of the swaggering, money-hungry Fred C. Dobbs, brilliantly played by Humphrey Bogart. Despite Howard's warnings about the dangers of greed, Dobbs is confident in his ability to take only the gold he sets out to find.

But Howard has seen it before and tells Dobbs and his friend that if they were to make a real strike, not even the threat of miserable death would keep them from trying to add ten thousand more, then twenty-five, and if they got twenty-five, then fifty thousand, and if fifty, a hundred. "It wouldn't be that way with me," Dobbs persists. "I swear it wouldn't. I'd take only what I set out to get, even if there was still a half a million dollars' worth lying around waitin' to be picked up." Despite Dobbs' confidence, Howard remains cynical. But he agrees to lead their trek into the mountains, where they sweat and toil in their quest for gold.

When they finally find a rich vein of gold, Dobbs' greed overcomes his earlier promises. He wants more: $50,000, at least. And the more gold they find, the more obsessive Dobbs becomes. He starts hiding his stash of gold from his partners. Obsession turns to paranoia as Dobbs descends further into a dungeon of greed, convinced his partners are out to kill him. "If ya know what's good for ya, ya won't monkey around with Fred C. Dobbs!" he warns.

But Dobbs' moral descent doesn't end there. His greed and fear lead down a path of no return, costing Dobbs more than he ever could have imagined. The most telling line in the film comes from the prospector, Howard: *"I know what gold does to men's souls."*

The Subtle Slavery of Greed

While the character study of Fred C. Dobbs remains one of the most entertaining depictions of greed in cinematic history, our real-life battles with this capital sin usually take a more subtle form. None of us are prospectors in the mountains searching for gold. And most people aren't *quite* as lacking in self-knowledge as Dobbs!

For most, *greed* and *avarice* are words we probably equate with stingy misers, corrupt brokers, or wicked pirates—Ebenezer Scrooge from *A Christmas Carol*, Gordon Gecko from *Wall Street*, or Captain Barbossa from *The Pirates of the Caribbean*. But these transparent examples of greed's corrupting effects could make us think we're safer from this vice than we really are.

Greed isn't usually obvious. It wears a mask of respectability that renders its presence in our lives difficult to detect. You may not be a miser or a pirate, but that doesn't mean you're off the hook. Greed has a way of gripping our hearts without us even realizing it. There are several truths we need to understand in order to recognize and unmask the sin of greed.

Greed Is a Root Sin

As we have seen, the Christian tradition has taught that all the seven deadly sins are root sins, and with good reason. But this is nowhere more explicit in Scripture than with the vice of greed.

> But those who desire to be rich fall into temptation, into a snare, into many senseless and harmful desires that plunge people into ruin and destruction. For the love of money is a root of all kinds of evils. It is through this craving that some have wandered away from the faith and pierced themselves with many pangs (1 Timothy 6:9–10).

"Avarice," says Billy Graham, "is probably the parent of more evil than all the other sins."[92] And Gregory said, "From avarice there spring treachery, fraud, deceit, perjury, restlessness, violence, and hardnesses of heart against compassion."[93] Greed is a mother sin, a root sin, a vice that spawns a deadly brood of venomous offspring.

Greed Is Disordered Love

Like all the capital sins, greed is also a disordered love. Rebecca DeYoung, following Aquinas, defines greed as, "an excessive love of or desire for money or any possession that money can buy."[94]

The Scriptures agree, commanding us to keep ourselves free from the *love of money*, not from money itself (see Hebrews 13:5). This is important, for it appropriately locates the problem of greed in the inordinate affections of our hearts, rather than in money or possessions *per se*. This means you can have a greed problem, even if you don't have a lot of money. The issue is not what you possess, but what possesses you.

Greed Is Deceptive and Destructive

The sin of greed deceives and destroys. As Paul teaches in the Hebrews passage referenced above, an inordinate craving for wealth leads to temptation and ensnares its victims in a cycle of foolish and harmful desires that "plunge people into ruin and destruction."

Don't miss the image: the desire for riches *ensnares*. A snare is a trap, effective because it is well-camouflaged. A skilled hunter baits his unwitting prey, keeping the snare hidden from view. The promise of wealth is a deceitful snare, a trap for unsuspecting souls.

Billy Graham tells a story of,

[A] party of tourists traveling through Death Valley, California [who] discovered the skeleton of a man who had died on the drifting dunes of the desert. Clutched in his bony hand was a chunk of mica whose pyrites, resembling gold, had deceived him. He had mistaken the yellow streaks in this rock for gold. On a scrap of paper under the skeleton were written the words, "Died rich." He had thought he was rich, but starved to death, lost and alone. Such is the deceitfulness of riches.[95]

Even worse, the deceitfulness of riches is fatally

combined with another lethal danger, one so great that Paul talks about it in terms of apostasy: "It is through this craving that some have wandered away from the faith and pierced themselves with many pangs." Much like the Hebrews 4 passage we discussed in the chapter on sloth, these words warn us that apparent Christians, caught in the snare of covetousness, sometimes forsake their profession of faith and the path of obedience. Biblical examples of this include Judas Iscariot, who betrayed Jesus for thirty pieces of silver (Matthew 26:15), and Paul's missionary companion Demas, who deserted Paul, "in love with this present world" (2 Timothy 4:10).

Greed Is Ultimately Unsatisfying

Ravi Zacharias tells the story of Guy de Maupassant, a nineteenth-century French author and father of the modern short story. His literary accomplishments brought great success and luxuriant wealth, including a yacht in the Mediterranean and a mansion on the coast of Normandy. But at the pinnacle of his career, his mental health broke down and Maupassant tried to kill himself, cutting his throat with a letter opener. He spent the rest of his short life in an asylum on the French Riviera and died at the age of forty-two, having penned his own epitaph: "I have coveted everything and taken pleasure in nothing."[96]

The sad story of Maupassant joins a litany of many others, confirming the wisdom of Ecclesiastes: "He who loves money will not be satisfied with money, nor he who loves wealth with his income; this also is vanity" (Ecclesiastes 5:10). The love of money will never satisfy. In the words of Peter Kreeft, trying to fill our hearts through avarice is "like trying to fill the Grand Canyon with marbles."[97]

We were made for something better. As C. S. Lewis has famously written, "If I find in myself a desire which no experience in this world can satisfy, the most probable explanation is that I was made for another world."[98]

The Contentment We Need

In contrast to the soul-piercing vice of avarice, the Scriptures teach us to cultivate the godly virtue of contentment. Of all the virtues, contentment may be the most difficult to cultivate for believers in the western world, for both external and internal factors work against us constantly. Externally, we live with a cultural pressure to accumulate more and more money, experiences, and stuff. Affluence is often considered the measure of success, and from childhood we are encouraged by families, teachers, and peers to pursue the American dream. Advertisements incessantly barrage us with products and experiences that we "need" or "deserve." Even if Christian virtues of stewardship and generosity were a part of our upbringing or heritage, just living in a culture of wealth has a way of shaping our expectations and desires. Add to this the subtle pressures of social media, where at the click of a mouse we're invited to compare our cars, homes, and family vacations with those of friends, family, and old classmates. Facebook, anyone?

But these external pressures would have little pull without the internal desires of our hearts. Our hearts are never neutral. They are spring-loaded with desire. Like a needle to a magnet, our hearts move constantly towards the achievements, possessions, and experiences we believe will make us happy.

Contentment, by contrast, is being satisfied with

what you have. Anyone can experience a measure of contentment on a temporary basis. But Christian contentment is something deeper, richer, and more enduring. Let's now consider three features of Christian contentment.

Contentment Isn't Dependent on Circumstances

Christian contentment is a satisfaction in Christ that transcends circumstances altogether. The best definition I've seen of this kind of contentment comes from Jeremiah Burroughs' classic book, *The Rare Jewel of Christian Contentment*. Burroughs defines Christian contentment as "that sweet, inward, gracious frame of spirit, which freely submits to and delights in God's wise and fatherly disposal in every condition."[99]

The best example of this in Scripture is the apostle Paul. Writing from a prison cell to the Philippian believers, Paul said, "I have learned in whatever situation I am to be content. I know how to be brought low, and I know how to abound. In any and every circumstance, I have learned the secret of facing plenty and hunger, abundance and need" (Philippians 4:11b–12).

This verse gives a second insight into contentment…

Contentment Is Something We Must Learn and Cultivate Over Time

"In any and every circumstance," wrote Paul, "*I have learned* the secret of facing plenty and hunger, abundance and need.*" I find this very encouraging. It shows that contentment was something Paul didn't always have. It didn't come naturally—he had to learn it. This gives me hope that I can learn contentment as well.

I also find this verse challenging, because it shows that contentment is something we have to learn *by experience*. Paul learned contentment in *any and every* circumstance by going through all kinds of *difficult* circumstances. So let's embrace this difficult but unchangeable reality—the only way to learn contentment in difficult circumstances is to live them: to be brought low, face hunger, and experience need.

In *The Hiding Place*, Corrie ten Boom recounts how she learned to thank God in every circumstance, even in the horror of Barracks 28 in the Ravensbrück concentration camp. The living conditions were inhumane. Fleas infested their barracks, and Corrie and her sister Betsie were just trying to survive and hold on to some fragment of faith, some little scrap of hope. One day Betsie remembered 1 Thessalonians 5:18, "Give thanks in all circumstances; for this is the will of God in Christ Jesus," and suggested that they should thank God for every single thing about the Barracks. They thanked God that they were together, that they still had a Bible, and even that they were in such crowded barracks, since this meant many could hear the Scriptures read aloud.

But Corrie would not thank God for the fleas. "There is no way even God can make me grateful for a flea!" she told Betsie.

"'Give thanks in all circumstances,'" Betsie replied. "It doesn't say 'in pleasant circumstances.' Fleas are part of this place where God has put us."

"And so we stood between piers of bunks and gave thanks for fleas," Corrie writes. "But this time I was sure Betsie was wrong."

She continues:

One evening I got back to the barracks late from a wood-gathering foray outside the walls. A light snow lay on the ground and it was hard to find the sticks and twigs with which a small stove was kept going in each room. Betsie was waiting for me, as always, so that we could wait through the food line together. Her eyes were twinkling.

"You're looking extraordinarily pleased with yourself," I told her.

"You know we've never understood why we had so much freedom in the big room," she said. "Well—I've found out."

That afternoon, she said, there'd been confusion in her knitting group about sock sizes and they'd asked the supervisor to come and settle it.

"But she wouldn't. She wouldn't step through the door and neither would the guards. And you know why?"

Betsie could not keep the triumph from her voice: "Because of the fleas! That's what she said, 'That place is crawling with fleas!'"

My mind rushed back to our first hour in this place. I remembered Betsie's bowed head, remembered her thanks to God for creatures I could see no use for.[100]

Contentment Comes from the Strength of Christ

If the kind of contentment that can thank God even for fleas sounds far beyond your reach, don't despair! For the Scriptures assure us that such contentment ultimately comes only through the supernatural strength of Christ.

Read Paul's words once more:

> I have learned in whatever situation I am to be
> content. I know how to be brought low, and I know
> how to abound. In any and every circumstance, I
> have learned the secret of facing plenty and hunger,
> abundance and need. *I can do all things through him
> who strengthens me.* (Philippians 4:11b–13)

Christian contentment isn't based on your temperament. It's not the result of strong willpower, or
self-induced detachment from the pains and pleasures
of life. It is a grace, a fruit of Christ's work in our hearts
and the strength-giving ministry of his Spirit. "Indeed,"
Burroughs observes, "in contentment there is a
compound of all graces."[101]

Pause for a moment to notice the amazing balance
of Scripture. Contentment is something we learn and
cultivate, yet it is also the result of Christ's strengthen-
ing our hearts. Some people say the Christian life is
all up to you, a matter of willpower, discipline, and
self-control. You have to do it yourself. On the other
side of the spectrum are those who say the Christian
life is simply letting Christ live his life in you. One side
under-emphasizes the work of Christ, while the other
under-emphasizes the necessity of effort on our part. The
reality is that it's both: contentment is a virtue you must
learn and cultivate, but you don't do this on your own.
Christ is the one who strengthens you. We only bear the
fruit of contentment as we abide in Christ; and as Martyn
Lloyd-Jones writes, "Abiding is a tremendously active
thing."[102]

The Promise that Sets Us Free

Having looked at the enslaving vice of greed and the opposing virtue of Christian contentment, what then is the path to freedom? How do we fight this root sin and cultivate the grace of contentment in its place? We get the answer from Hebrews 13:5–6. "Keep your life free from love of money, and be content with what you have, for he has said, 'I will never leave you nor forsake you.' So we can confidently say, 'The Lord is my helper; I will not fear; what can man do to me?'"

The key to contentment is in the conjunction that follows the command. "Keep your life free from love of money, and be content with what you have, *for…*" What follows is the reason we can obey this command: "for he has said, 'I will never leave you nor forsake you.'" This is the promise that sets us free. Notice two things about this promise.

First, it is the promise of God's presence. Learning contentment is not easy. Frankly, most of us probably are discontent to one degree or another. No one is exempt from this. And from a human perspective, our circumstances are sometimes difficult enough that contentment is completely elusive.

But look at this promise. It is not a promise that God will meet every material need, much less every want. There *are* assurances in Scripture that God faithfully provides for his people. But *this* is a promise for something more, something better: the promise of his presence with us. *"For he has said, 'I will never leave you, nor forsake you.'"*

And this makes all the difference in the world. This was the real secret for Corrie Ten Boom, who once said,

"You can never learn that Christ is all you need, until Christ is all you have."

Second, this promise gives us confidence and frees us from fear. That's why we read in verse 6: "So we can confidently say, 'The Lord is my helper; I will not fear; what can man do to me?'" The connection between verses 5 and 6 shows us that there is a close correlation between greed and fear on one hand, and contentment and confidence on the other. For God's Spirit, discerning the hidden secrets of our hearts, knows that greed is often rooted in a desire for security and control. And the opposite of security is fear—the fear of not having enough; the fear of losing control.

But this kind of fear comes from looking to people or things for what God alone can give. If my contentment is dependent on my circumstances, then anything that threatens the stability or security of those circumstances can become a source of fear and anxiety. But God's promise that he will never leave nor forsake me assures me that *God is on my side*—that he is my helper; that I will not be abandoned to the whims of people or the power of situations beyond my control. The Lord says he will be with his people, even in Ravensbrück, even when there are fleas, even when there is "tribulation, or distress, or persecution, or famine, or nakedness, or danger, or sword" (Romans 8:35).

And when the reality of this promise captures our hearts, when we are unshakably convinced that God is with us no matter what, then fear dissolves, and with it the powerful grip of greed.

Content with beholding his face,
My all to his pleasure resigned,
No changes of season or place
Would make any change in my mind:
While blest with a sense of his love,
A palace a toy would appear;
And prisons would palaces prove
If Jesus would dwell with me there. [103]

Examine and Apply

1. Do you think of yourself as a greedy or covetous person? Why or why not?
2. Now take a look at your checkbook and credit card statement. How much of your spending is on yourself? How much of your spending is discretionary (i.e., not on basic necessities of life)?
3. Do you struggle to be content with what you have? Do difficult circumstances steal your joy? What do the examples of the apostle Paul and Corrie Ten Boom teach us about contentment in Christ?
4. Can you think of other biblical promises that can help you in the struggle against covetousness?

Seven
GLUTTONY

If there is one sin of the Big Seven that we don't take very seriously, it's gluttony. Most of us would admit to occasional transgressions, perhaps over-stuffing at Thanksgiving or splurging on popcorn and soda at the movies. But gluttony usually falls off our vice lists. We may smugly agree it's an issue for overweight people, but not us. (How quickly we make snap judgments based on appearance, thinking little of the medical factors often involved in weight gain.)

But the sin of gluttony isn't just the sin of overeaters. It's the vice of a disordered appetite and the result of flabby thinking about what the Bible has to say about food—which happens to be a lot. In fact, food plays a surprisingly central role in the drama of redemption.

When God created the first humans, he placed them in a garden full of food. Humanity's fall into sin took place through an act of consumption, as Adam and Eve ate the forbidden fruit. In Exodus, the Passover (the most important redemptive event in the Old Testament) was commemorated with a special meal. Then the children of Israel complained about food and water, and God graciously provided manna from heaven and water from the rock.

When we get to the New Testament, Jesus scandalized the religious gatekeepers of the day with his eating habits. Unlike John the Baptist, Jesus didn't regularly fast. His inaugural miracle was turning ordinary water into fine wine at a wedding. Even worse, he frequently went to parties with tax collectors and prostitutes. In the early church, one of the most significant controversies was centered on practices of table fellowship: who can you eat with?

In the Book of Revelation, we read about the marriage supper of the Lamb and catch a glimpse of the future, where the tree of life will grow in the city of God, bearing twelve kinds of fruit, its leaves for the healing of the nations. And throughout Christian history, the church has recognized (with good biblical reasons) two food-related practices necessary to a full-flourishing life: the discipline of fasting and the sacrament of the Lord's Table. As you can see, one could write an entire book on the biblical theology of food.[104]

As we look at the sin of gluttony, we will anchor our study in the story of Jesus' feeding of the thousands in John 6. This story shows us that food is a gift—and like any gift, one we can idolize. But this story, along with Jesus' teaching, also shows how we can be rescued from the idolatry of food by feasting on Christ himself, the true bread from heaven.

The Gift of Food

Before we can think about the misuse of food through gluttony, we need to understand the gift of food itself. That food is God's gift is implicit in John 6 when "Lifting up his eyes, then, and seeing that a large crowd was coming toward him, Jesus said to Philip, 'Where are we to buy bread, so that these people may eat?'" (John 6:5). Jesus recognized physical hunger as a legitimate human need, and the rest of the story shows us how he multiplied a few loaves and fish to provide an abundance of food for the hungry multitude {vv 6–13}. Food is good: a created gift provided by God for the satisfaction of our physical needs.

We also learn this in the creation account, where God said to Adam, "Behold, I have given you every plant yielding seed that is on the face of all the earth, and every tree with seed in its fruit. You shall have them for food" (Genesis 1:29). After the flood, the scope of God's provision is enlarged so as to include animals: "Every moving thing that lives shall be food for you. And as I gave you the green plants, I give you everything" (Genesis 9:3).

The whole of Scripture affirms that food is not only God's gift, but also an evidence of his goodness to us. He not only gives food, he gives it in abundance and makes it pleasurable to eat. As the Psalmist wrote, "You cause the grass to grow for the livestock and plants for man to cultivate, that he may bring forth food from the earth and wine to gladden the heart of man, oil to make his face shine and bread to strengthen man's heart." (Psalm 104:14–15)

We should, therefore, receive our food with grateful hearts. When Jesus took the loaves, he gave thanks (John 6:11). And Paul both warns us against the dangers of food-related asceticism and reminds us of the importance of gratitude in receiving food.

Now the Spirit expressly says that in later times some will depart from the faith…who forbid marriage and require abstinence from foods that God created to be received with thanksgiving by those who believe and know the truth. For everything created by God is good, and nothing is to be rejected if it is received with thanksgiving, for it is made holy by the word of God and prayer" (1 Timothy 4:1a, 3–5).

Food is a gift and we must receive and enjoy it as such.

The Idolatry of Food

But John 6 also shows us the idolatry of food. We see this in verses 25–26: "When they found him on the other side of the sea, they said to him, 'Rabbi, when did you come here?' Jesus answered them, 'Truly, truly, I say to you, you are seeking me, not because you saw signs, but because you ate your fill of the loaves.'"

In an act of creative power and generosity, Jesus has fed the hungry multitude. But now he confronts the crowd because they come for more bread, while neglecting the greater significance of Jesus' true identity. Here is the Messiah, God in human flesh, present with his people. And the people are more concerned about dinner. They've made their bellies more important than God himself. They are guilty of idolatry.

We might not initially think of gluttony as having much to do with idolatry. Aquinas' definition of gluttony as "an immoderate appetite in eating and drinking"[105] seems to make more sense. But at its root, gluttony is about more than the amount of pizza one consumes. Gluttony is the prioritization of our bodily appetites over spiritual reality. Gluttony is a worship disorder. "A glutton," writes Frederick Buechner, "is one who raids the icebox for a cure for spiritual malnutrition."[106] Or in the words of Paul, many people "walk as enemies of the cross of Christ. Their end is destruction, their god is their belly, and they glory in their shame, with minds set on earthly things" (Philippians 3:18b–19).

"Gluttony is the sin of looking to food to satisfy the craving of our souls for security, a sense of well-being, comfort, and control over our lives.…Gluttony is a hunger for earthly things as a substitute for God himself."[107] Gluttony is the idolatry of food. But what does that look like? Let's consider three ways we can idolize food.

We Idolize Food by Giving It Too Much Importance

The classic biblical example of this is Esau, the son of Isaac. As the firstborn, Esau was heir of Isaac and of God's covenant promises to Abraham. The birthright was his.

But one day Esau, an outdoorsy "man's man," came in from a grueling day in the field and caught an appetizing whiff of his brother Jacob's homemade stew. And Esau had to have it. He wanted it so much that he offered to trade his birthright for a single bowl. Esau sold the most important thing in his life to satisfy the cravings of his growling stomach. While I don't personally know anyone who has made the conscious choice to trade God's promises for a bowl of stew, a great many Christians do end up cultivating appetites and habits of consumption that become so enslaving that they rob us of better things.

If Esau is the classic biblical example, perhaps Edmund Pevensie's inordinate hunger for Turkish

Delight is the best-known illustration from children's literature. The story is from C. S. Lewis' *The Lion, the Witch, and the Wardrobe*, where Edmund becomes the willing victim of a wicked Queen's seduction and lies. While attempting to gain information from Edmund, the Queen offers Edmund enchanted food.

> While he was eating the Queen kept asking him questions. At first Edmund tried to remember that it is rude to speak with one's mouth full, but soon he forgot about this and thought only of trying to shovel down as much Turkish Delight as he could, and the more he ate the more he wanted to eat, and he never asked himself why the Queen should be so inquisitive.

But the thing about "enchanted Turkish Delight" says Lewis, is that "anyone who had once tasted it would want more and more of it, and would even, if they were allowed, go on eating it till they killed themselves." Edmund's appetite becomes all-consuming, even after he is reunited with his sister Lucy, and learns how evil the White Witch is.

In spite of Lucy's warnings, "Edmund was already feeling uncomfortable from having eaten too many sweets, and when he heard that the Lady he had made friends with was a dangerous witch he felt even more uncomfortable. But he still wanted to taste that Turkish Delight again *more than he wanted anything else*."[108]

We Idolize Food by Treating It as an End in Itself

We pursue the satisfaction of our bodily appetites as if that's what life is about. This was the motto of the pagans:

"Let us eat and drink, for tomorrow we die" (1 Corinthians 15:32b). We see this attitude in Jesus' story about the rich fool who said to himself, "Soul, you have ample goods laid up for many years; relax, eat, drink, be merry," not knowing that his soul would be required of him that very night (Luke 12:19–20).

In *On Christian Doctrine*, one of the great classics of Christian literature, Augustine draws a careful distinction between *using* things and *enjoying* things. He pictures us as exiles longing to return from a foreign land to our own country, where our true happiness lies. We are therefore pilgrims: travelers on the journey home. As with all travelers, we need certain things to help us arrive at our destination, including refreshment along the way. But there's a problem, says Augustine, if we become so delighted with the pleasures of the journey that we're unwilling to finish it quickly. If we're not careful, we will lose interest in our home country, the place where true happiness awaits. When this happens, we've started to unduly enjoy the things that God intended to be used in helping us in our progress. And so as Augustine says, "If we wish to return to our home country, where alone we can be truly happy, we have to use this world, not enjoy it."[109]

Rebecca DeYoung finds the perfect illustration in a soldier's MRE. These "meals ready to eat" provide food in a way that's designed to help soldiers accomplish their mission. That doesn't mean they are tasteless. MREs include an entrée, but also a dessert or snack, a dry mix of coffee or something similar, along with packets of salt and pepper and Tabasco sauce. But the MRE is first and foremost functional. It's not a gourmet dinner, but a carefully packaged meal designed to provide soldiers in the field the necessary nutrition and sustenance needed to carry out their mission until they can return to base camp. And that means that soldiers have to subordinate their appetites to the demands of the mission. While the meals aren't unappetizing, their primary purpose isn't to satisfy every taste bud on every pallet, but to provide mission support with maximal efficiency and effectiveness. "Extending this analogy to our Christian life," writes DeYoung, "we can ask ourselves whether our eating habits are dedicated to serving our own pleasure or to serving our spiritual mission."[110]

We Idolize Food When We Become Slaves of Our Appetites

Slow down before writing this one off. You might think this only applies to people who obviously eat too much, suffer from an eating disorder, or are overweight. But the old theologians knew better and warned about five different expressions of gluttony. In a medieval epigram quoted by Aquinas, we are gluttonous if we eat, "hastily, sumptuously, too much, greedily, daintily."[111]

This is not to say that these five species of gluttony represent distinct and separate categories that can be backed up directly from Scripture. This is more in the category of biblically informed wisdom. When you realize that food can become an idol just like anything else, and that the way to avoid idolatry is to observe a balance between the enjoyment of food and the use of food, then these five become markers that ought to get our attention as possible indicators of idolatry.

Wrong use of food. If I regularly find myself

eating hastily, without due regard for God's good gift of food—that is, if I'm treating food merely as fuel—then my hastiness may be a sign that my attitude and approach toward food is drifting into idolatry.

Wrong enjoyment of food. In the same way, if I often eat sumptuously, or eat too much, or eat greedily, I should carefully check myself to see if I am seeking to find more gratification in food than I ought. It's all about the balance.

That leaves us with "daintily." What was Aquinas getting at there? Simply that you don't have to "overdo it" to idolize food. In *The Screwtape Letters*, Lewis discussed "the gluttony of Delicacy." Screwtape is a demon, writing a series of diabolical letters on the art of temptation and seduction to the junior tempter, Wormwood. In one letter, Screwtape describes how the demons have concentrated all their efforts on "gluttony of Delicacy, not gluttony of Excess" so that one old woman's "whole life is enslaved to this kind of sensuality, which is quite concealed from her by the fact that the quantities involved are small. But what do quantities matter, provided we can use a human *[Complaining]* belly and palate to produce querulousness, impatience, uncharitableness, and self-concern?"[112] This illustrates how easily we can be deceived. As Screwtape writes of the old woman, "At the very moment of indulging her appetite she believes that she is practising temperance."

There is clearly more than one way to be enslaved to your appetites. So, if you're thin and rarely struggle with over-eating, be careful how you judge. You may be just as enslaved to your appetites as someone with a larger jeans size.

The True Bread from Heaven

If gluttony really is a worship disorder, then the solution is to relocate our worship. Idolatry is always the attempt to find in a created thing what can only really be found in the Creator himself. We idolize food because we're trying to fill our souls by filling our bellies. But no matter how much we eat (or how little, or what kind, as the case may be), it will never satisfy our souls. It's not designed to. But there is a bread that satisfies, the true bread from heaven, Jesus himself. As Jesus said to the bread-demanding multitudes, "I am the bread of life; whoever comes to me shall not hunger, and whoever believes in me shall never thirst" (John 6:35).

What does Jesus mean when he calls himself the bread of life? What is this bread and how do we get it? And how do we use it to fight gluttony?

In the earlier part of John 6, Jesus speaks cryptically about the bread from heaven, alluding to the story of God's provision of manna for Israel. But in the course of his sermon, Jesus makes it clear. The bread Jesus gives is himself and the gift of life and joy that lasts forever.

> My father gives you the true bread from heaven. For the bread of God is he who comes down from heaven and gives life to the world (vv 32–33).

> I am the bread of life; whoever comes to me shall not hunger (v 35a).

> I am the living bread that came down from heaven. If anyone eats of this bread, he will live forever. And the bread that I will give for the life of the world is my flesh (v 51).[113]

Bread is a fitting image for Jesus and the gift he gives. It is made from grain that is *bruised* to become flour, which is *baked* to become bread, which is then *broken* and consumed so that it's converted into energy and gives life. This is what Jesus does for us. Jesus was bruised for us and faced the fire of affliction for us. He was "baked" for us in the suffering of the cross. Jesus gave over his body to be broken for us in death. And when we consume him — not physically, but spiritually — he gives us life. *"The bread that I will give for the life of the world is my flesh."*

We feast on this bread through faith. The crowds came to Jesus looking for a miracle, a work of God. But Jesus tells them the work of God is that you *believe* in the one whom God has sent (v 29). The subsequent verses show that it is through believing that we come to Christ, the true bread from heaven. "I am the bread of life; whoever *comes to me* shall not hunger, and whoever *believes in me* shall never thirst" (v 35). Only through faith do we receive the soul-satisfying life Jesus came to bring. This is what reorients our hearts away from idols to the true and living God.

This is all well and good, you might think, *but how does it help me fight the sin of gluttony? I get that Jesus is the bread of life. I see that I shouldn't idolize food. But I don't understand how knowing Jesus is the bread of life can actually help me with over-eating.* An answer is found in two practices that have been integral to Christian discipleship from the beginning: the discipline of fasting and the sacrament of the Lord's Supper.

The Discipline of Fasting

The first practice is fasting. Following his baptism, Jesus himself fasted for forty days and nights (Matthew 4:2).

And he taught his disciples to fast, saying,

> When you fast, do not look somber as the hypocrites
> do, for they disfigure their faces to show others
> they are fasting. Truly I tell you, they have received
> their reward in full. But when you fast, put oil on
> your head and wash your face, so that it will not be
> obvious to others that you are fasting, but only to
> your Father, who is unseen; and your Father, who
> sees what is done in secret, will reward you (Matthew
> 6:16–18).

This shows us, first, that Jesus expected his disciples
to fast. (He says *when*, not *if*, you fast.) But his teaching
also warns us not to fast to be seen by others. We should
fast, rather, with longing for the presence of Christ our
bridegroom (see Matthew 9:15). Fasting is therefore
closely connected to our desires. It is a way of forgoing
physical desire for the intensification of spiritual desire.
John Piper writes,

> If you don't feel strong desires for the manifesta-
> tion of the glory of God, it is not because you have
> drunk deeply and are satisfied. It is because you have
> nibbled so long at the table of the world. Your soul
> is stuffed with small things, and there is no room for
> the great. God did not create you for this. There is an
> appetite for God. And it can be awakened. I invite
> you to turn from the dulling effects of food and the
> dangers of idolatry, and to say with some simple fast:
> "This much, O God, I want you."[114]

The implications for fighting gluttony are obvious. Gluttony is a disordered desire for food, a mismanagement of our appetite. Fasting forces us to control our appetite. Gluttony is the attempt to fill the longings of our hearts with food that does not satisfy. When we fast, we temporarily give up food and train our spiritual appetite on Christ himself, thus loosing the stranglehold of food on our hearts.

The Sacrament of the Lord's Supper

The second Christian practice that realigns our longings is the regular celebration of the Lord's Supper. While Christians debate exactly how we ought to hold communion with Christ at the Table, almost all believers celebrate it in some form. My understanding conforms to the historic Reformed teaching that we hold a special fellowship with Christ at the table, through the ministry of the Spirit.

The Lord's Table is a means of grace, through which Christ nourishes and strengthens his church in the gospel. As the proclaimed Word nourishes us with the gospel *audibly*, so the communion table nourishes us with the gospel *visibly*. "For as often as you eat this bread and drink the cup, you proclaim the Lord's death until he comes" (1 Corinthians 11:26).

In fasting we remind our souls that our bodily appetites are not ultimate. At the Lord's Table, we taste and see that the Lord is good. The two practices together become regular, tangible ways both to train our appetites and to set our minds and hearts on the True Bread who satisfies our deepest needs, so that we can truly sing,

> *We taste Thee, O Thou living Bread,*
> *And long to feast upon Thee still;*
> *We drink of Thee, the Fountainhead,*
> *And thirst our souls from Thee to fill.*[115]

Examine and Apply

1. Do you regularly view food as God's good gift and thank him for it?
2. Have you idolized food by letting it become too important, or treating food as an end in itself? Have you become a slave to your own appetites?
3. Which species of gluttony best describes you: eating too much, too hastily, too greedily, too sumptuously, or too daintily?
4. How could the discipline of fasting help you fight a spiritual or emotional dependence on food? Have you ever thought about the Lord's Table as a tactile, sensory experience that can help you fix your appetite on Christ?

Eight
LUST

If there's one chapter in this book that immediately grabbed your attention, it's probably this one. Maybe you even turned here first. In the wake of the sexual revolution and with the proliferation of pornography through the Internet, Christians are wrestling more than ever with wayward sexual desires and a host of related issues.

In this chapter, I want to situate the problem of lust in the story of creation, fall, and redemption. Lust is a sin, a result of the fall. But sexual sin is a corruption and distortion of a created good. If we desire to cultivate healthy views of sexuality, we need to understand God's good intentions for it. And the only way to find freedom from the shackles of guilt and shame over sexual failures, along with hope and healing for sexual brokenness and disappointment, is through the redemptive power of Christ.

Creation: God's Intentions for Sex

First, it's essential for us to see the basic goodness of sexuality as a gift created by God. If we don't understand sex in relationship to God's purpose for it, we'll be sure to misuse it—either denigrating and despising it on one hand, or idolizing and abusing it on the other. But if we understand the biblical perspective on sexuality, we can then begin to understand how lust distorts God's purpose for sex and how the gospel in turn redeems and restores.

We can summarize this perspective with two statements: First, the body was made *by* the Lord: therefore, sex is good. Second, the body was made *for* the Lord: therefore, sex is not ultimate.

Paul speaks from this perspective in his explanation of Christian sexual ethics in 1 Corinthians 6. In verse 13, he seems to be quoting one of the slogans used in Corinth to justify unbridled sensuality, even prostitution. "'Food is meant for the stomach and the stomach for food'—and God will destroy both one and the other. The body is not meant for sexual immorality, but for the Lord, and the Lord for the body" (1 Corinthians 6:13). As one commentary notes, "The libertines in Corinth were evidently using this as a slogan to show that sensual indulgence was as natural and necessary to the body, as food was to the stomach."[116]

Paul disagrees, but not in the way we might think. He doesn't say, "No, the body is bad. Sex is bad. You're made for spiritual pleasure, not bodily pleasure. Focus on the spiritual, not the physical." But Paul doesn't denigrate the body; he elevates it. He says, "The body is not meant for sexual immorality, *but for the Lord, and the Lord for the body.*"

Paul's words, rooted in a robust theology of creation, steer a straight course between unchecked hedonism and stern asceticism. Paul, in line with the rest of Scripture, teaches that God created the material world and instituted the marriage relationship, pronouncing it "very good"

(Genesis 1:31). In contrast to religious systems that teach that good and evil coexist eternally (often equating evil with matter, and good with the nonmaterial or spiritual), Christianity affirms the inherent goodness of the created world in all its physicality and materiality. Nature, bodies, food, sex: these are goods created by God as gifts for his creatures.

When God created human beings *in his image*, he created them male and female (Genesis 1:27). He created the institution of marriage and told the first couple to have sex! "And God said to them, 'Be fruitful and multiply and fill the earth.'" (Genesis 1:28a). Marriage is one man and one woman committed to one another for life. And in the context of marriage, having sexual intercourse is both God's mandate and his gift.

Unfortunately, the primary message Christians sometimes send about sex is negative. Yet sex is not sinful. Sex was God's idea. He invented it. The body is made *by* the Lord and marriage was instituted by him as well: therefore, sex is good.

But these truths are balanced by remembering that the body is also made *for* the Lord. Therefore, while sex in marriage is *good*, it is not *ultimate*. It is a subordinate good, intended for our good and God's glory. And subordinate to the ultimate intention of glorifying God are three interrelated purposes for sex: the consummation of the marriage union (Genesis 2:24), the procreation of children (Genesis 1:28), and the mutual pleasure and delight of a husband and wife (Proverbs 5:18–19; 1 Corinthians 7:1–5).

The biblical theology of creation, the body, marriage, and sexuality sets sexual desire in its proper place. Sexual desire is meant to be a servant, not a sovereign. As Lewis said, "No natural feelings are high or low, holy or unholy, in themselves. They are all holy when God's hand is on the rein. They all go bad when they set up on their own and make themselves into false gods."[117] When we allow desire to usurp the throne, it becomes a tyrant.

But treating sexual satisfaction as ultimate is exactly what lust does. Lust, like the other deadly sins, is a worship problem. Lust is idolatry, the result of the Fall.

Fall: The Idolatry of Sex

The taproot of sinful sexual behavior is lust. But lust needs to be distinguished from normal and healthy sexual desire. As we've already seen, sex itself is not sinful, and neither is sexual desire. Sexual desire is normal and a part of being human. You can have sexual desires, feel sexual attraction, and even experience sexual temptation without sinning through lust. So, what is lust? *Lust is a disordered and idolatrous sexual desire that is both enslaving and destructive.*

Lust Is a Disordered Desire

In the chapter on anger we briefly discussed *concupiscence*, a somewhat dated term for any strong desire that leads us into sin. The most classic expression of concupiscence is probably sexual lust. In fact, the Greek word translated *concupiscence* in the King James Version refers to sinful sexual desire in 1 Thessalonians 4:5. But, as we saw before, this word means not just desire, but *inordinate* desire.

On one level, lust is an *excessive* desire for sexual pleasure: wanting sexual fulfillment too much or pursuing it in ways or relationships forbidden by God. But from another angle, lust is a *defective* desire, for it wants not too much, but too little. Lust desires sexual pleasure minus the kind of relationship sex was designed for in the first place.

> The monstrosity of sexual intercourse outside marriage is that those who indulge in it are trying to isolate one kind of union (the sexual) from all the other kinds of union which were intended to go along with it and make up the total union. The Christian attitude does not mean that there is anything wrong about sexual pleasure, any more than about the pleasure of eating. It means that you must not isolate that pleasure and try to get it by itself, any more than you ought to try to get the pleasures of taste without swallowing and digesting, by chewing things and spitting them out again.[118]

Lust strips sex from the context of marriage, reducing it to the satisfaction of a bodily craving. And the more entrenched the acceptance of lust becomes in our culture, the more depersonalizing and dehumanizing it becomes, often divorcing sex from any kind of meaningful relationship at all. As actor Steve Carell quipped, when presenting the award for best sound editing at the 79th Oscars: "Sound editing is very much like sex. It's usually done alone, late at night, surrounded by electronic gadgets." Everyone laughed, of course. But it's not funny, it's sad. It reveals the dark isolation and soul-numbing loneliness of lust. Lust seizes a created good (sex) that is intended for the nourishment of a committed life-long relationship in marriage, and shreds it of love and meaning.

Lust Is an Idolatrous Desire

Where does this disordered desire come from? Why do we lust? In her essay on the deadly sins, Dorothy Sayers said "there are two main reasons for which people fall into the sin of luxuria." On one hand, people may fall into lust because of the "sheer exuberance of animal spirits." When this is the case, "a sharp application of the curb may be all that is needed to bring the body into subjection and remind it of its proper place." This is probably where many of the remedies prescribed against lust originated: go for a hard run; take a cold shower; fast from rich food; *et cetera*.

But Sayers says there is a second reason for lust. "When philosophies are bankrupt and life appears without hope—men and women may turn to lust in sheer boredom and discontent, trying to find in it some stimulus that is not provided by the drab discomfort of their mental and physical surroundings."[119]

We see an example of this in Albert Camus' novel *The Fall*, the story of a man named Clamence whose slow descent into excessive hedonism left him with a hollow emptiness inside. In one place Clamence says, "Because I longed for eternal life, I went to bed with harlots and drank for nights on end. In the morning, to be sure, my mouth was filled with the bitter taste of the mortal state."[120]

At its root, lust is an attempt to use sexual satisfaction to fill the void in one's soul. Lust is the idolatry of sex.

Lust Is an Enslaving Desire

Paul says, "'All things are lawful for me,' but not all things are helpful. 'All things are lawful for me,' but I will not be *dominated* by anything" (1 Corinthians 6:12). In Titus 3:3, he reminds us that we were "once foolish, disobedient, led astray, *slaves* to various passions and pleasures." Lust is a dominating, enslaving desire.

One reason lust holds people captive is because it so easily becomes habitual. Even non-Christian psychologists are beginning to talk about sexual addictions in much the same language used to describe drug and alcohol addictions. But Augustine discovered this centuries ago, when he likened his slavery to lust as a chain.

> It was no iron chain imposed by anyone else that fettered me, but the iron of my own will. The enemy had my power of willing in his clutches, and from it had forged a chain to bind me. The truth is that disordered lust springs from a perverted will; when lust is pandered to, a habit is formed; when habit is not checked, it hardens into compulsion. These were like interlinking rings forming what I have described as a chain, and my harsh servitude used it to keep me under duress.[121]

Notice the four links in Augustine's chain: perverted will, disordered lust, habit, and compulsion. These links perfectly describe the psychological dynamics of addiction. It begins with a distortion in the will, a choice to taste the forbidden fruit. Having tasted the fruit, deeper desires follow; these indulged become habit forming. Soon, the addict seeks a fix, driven not by the freedom of desire, but the slavery of compulsion. "Addiction is a dramatic portrait of some main dynamics of sin, a stage show of warped longings, split wills, encumbered liberties, and perverse attacks on one's own well-being."[122]

Lust Is a Destructive Desire

Lust is a destructive desire because it's a sin against one's own body: "Flee from sexual immorality. Every other sin a person commits is outside the body, but the sexually immoral person sins against his own body" (1 Corinthians 6:18). The physical results of unbridled debauchery are obvious: syphilis, gonorrhea, chlamydia, and more.

But I think Paul refers to something more insidious and destructive than an STD. For sexual sins distort, for selfish ends, the good God intended for the purpose of self-giving love in the union of marriage. Such a false use of sex cuts across the grain of flourishing sexuality and thus leads not to the flourishing, but the diminishing of the self. In Lewis' words, "Lechery means not simply forbidden pleasure but loss of the man's unity."[123]

Lust is also destructive because it leads to other sins. The obvious examples are sinful sexual behaviors: fornication, adultery, prostitution, rape, etc. But lust is a vice that breeds other sins as well. As Gregory writes, "From lust are generated blindness of mind, inconsiderateness, inconstancy, precipitation, self-love, hatred of God, affection for this present world, but dread or despair of that which is to come."[124]

And apart from redemption, lust is a sin that damns and destroys forever. Paul's words could not be clearer: "Do you not know that the unrighteous will not inherit the kingdom of God? Do not be deceived: neither the sexually immoral, nor idolaters, nor adulterers, nor men who practice homosexuality... will inherit the kingdom of God" (1 Corinthians 6:9–10).

Redemption: How Christ Rescues Sexual Sinners

But the good news is that Christ rescues sexual sinners. His redemptive power promises pardon for our sexual transgressions, healing for our sexual brokenness, and glorious restoration for our fractured sexual selves. The gospel addresses our sexual lives in all its dimensions: past, present, and future.

Grace for the Past

I'm so thankful that after the litany of sins that bar people from God's kingdom in 1 Corinthians 6:9–10, Paul goes on to say, "And such were some of you. But you were washed, you were sanctified, you were justified in the name of the Lord Jesus Christ and by the Spirit of our God" (1 Corinthians 6:11).

Some readers will especially need this assurance. Perhaps you are paralyzed by guilt over your past. Maybe you had sex outside of marriage or committed adultery. Perhaps you have cultivated an unhealthy thought life or a sexual addiction. Maybe this finds you winning the war against lust, but losing occasional battles along the way. You know the sins. You know the failures. Sometimes you feel that you'll never be free of them. The guilt eats you alive.

But here is good news: if you are in Christ, you have been washed, sanctified, and justified. In him, you are clean. You've been given a new record. Grace covers all your sins, all your past.

Martin Luther, a sinful and imperfect man in many ways, both before and after becoming a Christian, was sometimes haunted by his sins and plagued with guilt.

But he also knew the relief found only in Christ. Luther said, "We are not to look upon our sins as insignificant trifles. On the other hand, we are not to regard them as so terrible that we must despair."

> Learn to believe that Christ was given, not for [trivial] and imaginary transgressions, but for mountain-ous sins; not for one or two, but for all; not for sins that can be discarded, but for sins that are stubbornly ingrained. Practice this knowledge and fortify yourself against despair…. Say with confidence: "Christ, the Son of God, was given not for the righteous, but for sinners. If I had no sin I should not need Christ."[125]

Whatever your sins may be, there is grace, forgiveness, and pardon for you in Christ. Like Bunyan's pilgrim, the burden of your sin and guilt can be loosed from your shoulders at the cross. And you can say, with the old hymn writer,

> *Well may the accuser roar*
> *Of sins that I have done!*
> *I know them all and thousands more,*
> *Jehovah knoweth none!*[126]

Guidance for the Present

But the Scriptures give not only grace for the past, but guidance for the present. Christ not only forgives; he also renews and restores. He wants what is best for us, including what's best for our sex lives. But the only way to secure his best is for sex to resume its proper place. We must replace vice with virtue: lust with chastity. "(Sensual love)," says Lewis, "ceases to be a devil when it ceases to be a god…So many things—nay every real *thing*—is good if only it will be humble and ordinate."[127]

We cultivate the virtue of chastity through the practice of two basic disciplines.

Abstinence. The first practice is to flee sexual sin. This is *the discipline of abstinence*. "Flee sexual immorality" (1 Corinthians 6:18). "So flee youthful passions" (2 Timothy 2:22a). "For this is the will of God, your sanctification: that you abstain from sexual immorality" (1 Thessalonians 4:3). Like Joseph who fled from Potiphar's wife, so we ought to run from every temptation and occasion for sexual sin. "But among you there must not be even a hint of sexual immorality, or of any kind of impurity, or of greed, because these are improper for God's holy people" (Ephesians 5:3, NIV).

A few years ago we noticed a faint smell of gas in our house. We wanted to be careful, so I called our gas company and asked them to come take a look. They did, sending a man who checked every possible place where there could be the tiniest trace of gas. Several times he made reference to the company's "zero-tolerance" policy. If there is any gas leak at all, they shut things down. By the time he left, I had a list of four repairs that needed to be made, including a new cook-top, because every one of the valves was leaking. They weren't leaking much. But they were leaking a little and the repairman said, in effect, "We cannot leave even a hint of gas in this house." The Lord wants us to be just as thorough in removing the tiniest traces of sexual sin from our lives. Not even a hint should remain.

Marriage. The second practice is for the married: be faithful to your spouse. This means not only that you shouldn't sleep with someone else, but also that you should faithfully meet the sexual needs of your husband or wife. This is *the discipline of fidelity*.

Paul's teaching in 1 Corinthians 7 reveals three aspects of fidelity. Fidelity means: (1) *exclusivity*: reserving sex for your spouse and no one else (v 2); (2) *reciprocity*: deferring to your spouse's needs and desires (v 3–4); and (3) *regularity*: refusing to deprive one another of sexual relations, except for the rare, mutually agreed upon purpose of devoting yourselves to prayer (v 5).

Glory for the Future

Some readers will bring to this chapter not so much the guilt of sexual failures, but the disappointment of unfulfilled desires. If you are *not* married, whether by circumstances or by choice, and are fighting for chastity, reading Paul's prescriptions for regular sexual intercourse in marriage could feel more frustrating than helpful. Perhaps you *are* married, but your spouse is unable or unwilling to have sex as often as you'd like. Or maybe you *were* married, but are now widowed or divorced. Any of these situations could leave you feeling a fair bit of frustration regarding sex.

But the Scriptures speak to this as well. "The body is not meant for sexual immorality, but for the Lord, and the Lord for the body. *And God raised the Lord and will also raise us up by his power*" (1 Corinthians 6:13b–14). Don't miss the last phrase: God will raise our bodies by his power. There is glory for the future. We will be raised and glorified, transformed by the sight of Christ in all of his kingly glory. "Dear friends, now we are children of God, and what we will be has not yet been made known. But we know that when Christ appears, we shall be like him, for we shall see him as he is" (1 John 3:2).

One of the enemy's lies is that you cannot have a fully satisfying life without sexual fulfillment. But this makes the body and its experiences ultimate. The truth is that the eternal joy that awaits is incomparable to any heartache, frustration, or disappointment you may face, *or* any sexual pleasure you could possibly experience. "The happiness which God designs for his higher creatures," said Lewis, "is the happiness of being freely, voluntarily united to him and to each other in an ecstasy of love and delight, compared with which the most rapturous love between a man and woman on this earth is mere milk and water."[128]

Tim Keller tells a story about,

> A king who went out in his village to meet his subjects. Everybody said he was a magical king. A beggar sitting by the road lifted up his bowl expecting the king to give him some money. Instead, the king asked the beggar to give him something. Well, the beggar had a bowl of rice. That's all he had. Taken aback, the beggar just pulled out three grains of rice and put them in the king's hand. The king said, "Thank you," and went on. When [the beggar] looked down, he found three gold nuggets in his bowl. He looked up, and he said, "If only I had given him everything."

And then Keller adds, "If you give God your sexual desires, I tell you they'll be reborn."[129]

Conclusion

My favorite book by C. S. Lewis is *The Great Divorce*, which I discussed briefly in the chapter on pride. The book is a theological fantasy about a group of hellish ghosts who are given a holiday to the borderland of Heaven. They encounter astonishing wonders: daisies more solid than diamonds, a waterfall that thunders like "the revelry of a whole college of giants laughing, dancing, singing, roaring at their high works,"[130] and solid gold apples too heavy to lift.

Though the specters on this excursion are residents of the endless grey city of Hell, they are given the opportunity to leave their vices behind for the solid joys and lasting treasures of Heaven (remember, it's a theological *fantasy*). But all refuse, save one, a dark, oily ghost tormented by a little red lizard that sits on his shoulders, "twitching its tail like a whip and whispering" seductions in his ear.

A flaming Spirit offers to slay the lizard, but the ghost hesitates. Killing the lizard would be too drastic, too painful. Surely trying to control it is better? Or maybe it will go to sleep? But even though the ghost fears the angel's blazing touch, he eventually concedes and cries out "God help me. God help me."

The angel seizes the reptile, breaks its back, and flings it to the ground. And then something amazing happens: the ghost is transformed into an immense man, while the lizard is reborn as a great silvery white stallion.

> In joyous haste the young man leaped upon the horse's back. Turning in his seat he waved a farewell, then nudged the stallion with his heels. They were

off before I knew well what was happening. There was riding if you like! I came out as quickly as I could from among the bushes to follow them with my eyes; but already they were only like a shooting star far off on the green plain, and soon among the foothills of the mountains. Then, still like a star, I saw them winding up, scaling what seemed impossible steeps, and quicker every moment, till near the dim brow of the landscape, so high that I must strain my neck to see them, they vanished, bright themselves, into the rose-brightness of that everlasting morning.

The creative power of this story captures my imagination and steels my heart with the startling truth that anyone who denies self, takes up the cross, and follows Jesus, will in turn discover true life and joy beyond their wildest dreams. "For whoever would save his life will lose it, but whoever loses his life for [Jesus'] sake and the gospel's will save it" (Mark 8:35).

Though the lizards of lust, along with the lions, toads, and wolves of pride, envy, greed, and the rest must die, we will lose nothing in their mortification. For joy will arise phoenix-like from the ashes. The happiness we ardently desired but vainly sought after in lesser things will be given in measures greater than we can conceive. As Lewis said, "Lust is a poor, weak, whimpering whispering thing compared with that richness and energy of desire which will arise when lust has been killed."

We were made for glory. Sin has robbed us of this destiny. But the gospel declares that a rescue operation is underway. Commissioned in his Father's love, the Eternal Son has faced off against our mortal enemies once and for all. He fought the good fight and accomplished redemption. Through death he defeated death itself, and with it the sin that held us captive. He now reigns in the power of his resurrection while his Spirit runs through history bringing forgiveness and healing, hope and transformation, to all who believe.

"The old has passed away; behold, the new has come" (2 Corinthians 5:17).

Examine and Apply

1. Do you have a healthy and biblical view of sexuality? Do you view sex as a gift or a curse? Does your thinking about sex need to be rewired?

2. Are your sexual desires disordered? For example… Do you desire sexual fulfillment in ways that are forbidden in Scripture? Are you enslaved by your desires? Are you indulging in lustful glances, thoughts, fantasies, or habits? Do you lack self-control? Do you take seriously the scriptural warnings about the danger of sexual sin?

3. Have you learned to take your guilt to the cross? Whatever the haunting sins of your past, take them to Jesus now. Then recommit yourself to the Christian practices of abstinence and fidelity.

4. How could the doctrines of resurrection and glorification help you in dealing with sexual disappointment and frustration?

Acknowledgments

"Acknowledgments," according to the wry and witty essayist Joseph Epstein, "are the literary equivalent of tipping, but with Monopoly money." So, here I am dishing out golden five hundred dollar bills to the friends and loved ones whose love, generosity, and sacrifice made this book possible.

This has been my third partnership with Kevin Meath, an extraordinary editor, from whom I've learned a lot about writing. Thanks for the opportunity to publish another book with Cruciform Press.

Special thanks also to Bob Lepine, for writing the Foreword (and on short notice) and to Brian Croft, for offering a helpful suggestion that improved the chapter on Wrath.

Thanks to the elders and members of Fulkerson Park Baptist Church, where I serve as lead pastor, for granting me a paid writing leave in the summer of 2014. I am grateful for their enthusiastic support to my writing.

A shout out to my wonderful in-laws, Marion and Linda Ivey, who cheerfully welcomed our family of six into their home for an entire month. Benjamin Franklin once said, "Guests, like fish, begin to smell after three days." If Marion and Linda felt this way, they never let on. Instead, they made the summer a delight for Holly and the kids, while I feverishly banged out a manuscript at a nearby Starbucks.

High fives to Holly, my rock star of a wife, for never flinching when I say, "I have an idea for a book," even though, after three previous books, she now knows the cost. Thanks for loving me through all the highs and lows of writing.

Finally, I've dedicated this book to my dear friend Tim Smith, who (apart from Holly) knows more of my dirt than anyone else alive. Thanks for praying for, talking to, exhorting, and encouraging me. It's good to have a brother fighting alongside me in the trenches.

Endnotes

1. Brian G. Hedges, *Licensed to Kill: A Field Manual for Mortifying Sin* (Cruciform Press, 2011).

2. Cornelius Plantinga Jr., *Not the Way It's Supposed to Be: A Breviary of Sin* (Eerdmans, 1995) p 9.

3. For a contemporary translation see David Brakke, trans. Evagrius of Pontus: *Talking Back: A Monastic Handbook for Combating Demons* (Cistercian, 2009). Despite calling the thoughts "demons," Evagrius didn't propose a well-developed doctrine of Satan or demons.

4. See *John Cassian: The Conferences,* Trans., Boniface Ramsey (Newman Press, 1997) and John Cassian: The Institutes Trans., Boniface Ramsey (Newman Press, 2000). The quotation on natural and unnatural vices is from The Conferences, p 183.

5. John Calvin, *Institutes of the Christian Religion*, Book IV, Ch. xvii, Section 49, Ed., John T. McNeil, Trans., Ford L. Battles (Westminster Press, 1960) p 1427. Emphasis added.

6. Saint Gregory the Great, *Morals on the Book of Job*, Edited by Paul A. Böer, Sr. (Veritatis Splendor Publications, 2012) Book XXXI.

7. On mortal and venial sin, see *Catechism of the Catholic Church*, Part 3, Article 8, Section IV. (The Wanderer Press, 1994) pp 454-456. The seven deadly sins are called "capital sins" in the Catechism, and are discussed in Part 3, Article 8, Section V, p 457.

8. John T. Mabray, *The Seven Deadly Sins and Spiritual Transformation* (Xulon Press, 2010) p xiii.

9. Dorothy L. Sayers, in her introduction to Dante's *The Divine Comedy II: Purgatory* (Penguin Books, 1955) p 65. Emphasis orig.

10. John Cassian: *The Conferences*, p 183.

11. Gregory, Book XXXI, Ch. 45.87-88.

12. Rebecca Konyndyk DeYoung, *Glittering Vices: A New Look at the Seven Deadly Sins and Their Remedies* (Brazos Press, 2009) p 33. I am indebted to DeYoung not only for her excellent historical overview of the seven deadly sins, but also for providing the genesis for much of my thinking and reading.

13. Ibid, p 14. **14.** Ibid, p 34. **15.** Ibid, p 14. **16.** Ibid, p 21.

17. What DeYoung calls "the misguided pursuit of happiness" (p. 38). For more on the seven deadly sins in relationship to disordered loves, see David K. Naugle, *Reordered Love, Reordered Lives: Learning the Deep Meaning of Happiness* (Eerdmans, 2008).

18. Saint Augustine, *The Confessions*, Book II, Ch. 6.12-14, Trans.

Maria Boulding (New City Press, 1997) pp 70-71.

19. C. S. Lewis, *The Collected Letters of C. S. Lewis, Volume II: Books, Broadcasts, and the War: 1931-1949*, Ed. Walter Hooper (HarperOne, 2004), pp 122-125. Emphasis original.

20. John Owen, *Overcoming Sin and Temptation*, Ed. Kelly M. Kapic, Justin Taylor (Crossway, 2006), p 47.

21. Ibid., p 131. Emphasis original.

22. This is not to deny the reality of personality challenges that are rooted in biological or genetic conditions. These too, however, find their roots in man's fall into sin and can often be addressed to some degree by the sanctifying grace of God.

23. Gregory, Book XXXI, Ch. 45 **24.** Ibid.

25. C. S. Lewis, *Mere Christianity* (HarperOne, 1952, 1980) p 121-122.

26. David E. Garland, *1 Corinthians*, Baker Exegetical Commentary on the New Testament (Baker Academic, 2003), p 618.

27. Gordon D. Fee, *The First Epistle to the Corinthians*, New International Commentary on the New Testament (Eerdmans, 1987), p 637.

28. John Piper, *The Purifying Power of Living by Faith in FUTURE GRACE* (Multnomah Books, 1995) pp 94-95.

29. Plantinga, p 84.

30. Saint Augustine, *The City of God*, Book XIV, Ch. 28, in Nicene and Post-Nicene Fathers, vol. 2, Edited by Philip Schaff (Hendrickson Publishers, 1887, 2004) p 282.

31. C. S. Lewis, "The Shoddy Lands," in *Of Other Worlds: Essays and Stories* (Harcourt Brace & Company, 1975), pp 99-106.

32. C. S. Lewis, *The Great Divorce* (HarperOne, 1946, 1973) p 75. Emphasis original.

33. Peter Kreeft, *Back to Virtue* (Ignatius Press, 1992) p 100.

34. Gerard Reed, *C. S. Lewis Explores Vice and Virtue* (Beacon Hill Press of Kansas City, 2001) p 28. Emphasis original.

35. Calvin, p 269, n. 50.

36. Jonathan Edwards, *Religious Affections*, Ed., John E. Smith, The Works of Jonathan Edwards, vol. 2 (Yale Univ. Press, 1959) p 312.

37. Quoted in Kreeft, p 99.

38. Owen, p 282. Emphasis original.

39. Piper, p 97.

40. Elizabeth C. Clephane, "Beneath the Cross of Jesus," 1868.

41. Quoted in Jeff Cook, *The Seven Deadly Sins and the Beatitudes* (Zondervan, 2008), p 55.

42. Quoted in Gerard Reed, *C. S. Lewis on Vice and Virtue* (Beacon Hill Press of Kansas City, 2001) pp 36-37.

43. Thomas Aquinas, *Summa Theologica*, II-II. Q. 36. Art. 1, Translated by Fathers of the English Dominican Province (Coyote Canyon Press, Kindle Edition, 2010). Aquinas was quoting John of Damascus, a seventh century Syrian monk.

44. Aristotle, *Rhetoric*, Book II, Ch. 9; quoted in Solomon Schimmel, *The Seven Deadly Sins: Jewish, Christian, and Classical Reflections on Human Psychology* (Oxford University Press, 1997) p 80.

45. Jonathan Edwards, *Ethical Writings*, Ed. Paul Ramsey, *The Works of Jonathan Edwards*, vol. 8 (Yale University Press, 1989) p 219.

46. Frederick Buechner, *Wishful Thinking: A Seeker's ABC* (HarperOne, 1993) p 24.

47. Reed, p 35

48. Joseph Epstein, *Envy: The Seven Deadly Sins* (New York Public Library Lectures in Humanities) (Oxford University Press, 2003) p 18.

49. Dorothy L. Sayers, "The Other Six Deadly Sins" in *The Whimsical Christian: 18 Essays* (Macmillan Publishing, 1978) pp 171-172.

50. Quoted in DeYoung, p 45.

51. Quoted by Billy Graham, *The 7 Deadly Sins* (Zondervan, 1955) p 44.

52. Rebecca Manley Pippert, *A Heart for God: Learning from David through the Tough Choices of Life* (InterVarsity Press, 2002) pp 70-72.

53. Graham, p 41-42.

54. Plantinga, p 157.

55. William R. White, *Fatal Attractions: Sermons on the Seven Deadly Sins* (Abingdon, 1992) p 31.

56. C. S. Lewis, *The Last Battle* (Macmillan, 1956) Chapter 13.

57. Quoted by A. S. Bryant in "The Deadly Sins/Envy: The Sin of Families and Nations," 7/18/1993, *The New York Times*. Available online at: http://www.nytimes.com/books/99/06/13/specials/byatt-sins.html .

58. Saint Augustine, *De Catech Rud.* 8, quoted in John Burnaby, *Amor Dei: A Study of the Religion of St. Augustine* (Wipf & Stock Publishers, 1938, 2007) p 171.

59. Edwards, *Ethical Writings*, p 224.

60. The title of a famous sermon by Thomas Chalmers, "The Expulsive Power of a New Affection," reprinted in Andrew Watterson Blackwood, comp., *The Protestant Pulpit: An Anthology of Master Sermons from the Reformation to Our Own Day* (Abingdon, 1947), pp 50-62.

61. Aristotle, *The Nicomachean Ethics*, Book IV, Ch. V, Trans. J. A. K. Thompson, (Penguin Classics, 2003) p 101.
62. Sayers, p 67.
63. C. S. Lewis, *Letters to Malcolm: Chiefly on Prayer* (Harcourt, 2002) p 97.
64. Robert D. Jones, *Uprooting Anger: Biblical Help for a Common Problem* (P & R Publishing, 2005) p 29. In Jones' book, these are headings followed by further explanation. I have changed the use of capitalization. **65.** Ibid, p 15.
66. Anthony C. Thiselton, *The First Epistle to the Corinthians*, The New International Greek Testament Commentary (Eerdmans, 2000) p 1053.
67. Jay E. Adams, *The Christian Counselor's Manual* (Zondervan, 1986), p 349.
68. R. Scott Clark, "Concupiscence: Sin and the Mother of Sin," *Modern Reformation*, Nov/Dec 2001. Volume 10. Issue 6. Available online at: http://www.modernreformation.org/default. php?page=articledisplay&var2=361 . Accessed 71/2014.
69. Gregory, Book XXXI, Ch. 45.88.
70. Buechner, p 2.
71. Quoted by DeYoung, p 117.
72. Lewis, *Mere Christianity*, p 93.
73. Piper uses this illustration in a slightly different context in John Piper, *A Hunger for God: Desiring God through Fasting and Prayer* (Crossway, 1997) p 149.
74. Horatio Spafford, "It is Well with My Soul," 1873.
75. Sayers, *The Divine Comedy II*, p 209.
76. Sayers, *The Whimsical Christian: 18 Essays*, p 176.
77. As told by Solomon Schimmel, *The Seven Deadly Sins: Jewish, Christian, and Classical Reflections on Human Psychology* (Oxford University Press, 1997) p 200.
78. Schimmel, p 193.
79. Sayers, *The Whimsical Christian: 18 Essays*, p 176
80. R. R. Reno, *Fighting the Noonday Devil – and Other Essays Personal and Theological* (Eerdmans, 2011) p 3.
81. Peter T. O'Brien, *The Letter to the Hebrews*, Pillar New Testament Commentary (Eerdmans, 2002) p 206.
82. DeYoung, p 79.
83. Reno, p 3.
84. John Owen, *Overcoming Sin and Temptation*, Ed. Kelly M. Kapic, Justin Taylor (Crossway, 2006). Owen deals with this in chapter 10 of *The Nature and Power of Indwelling Sin*. All the quotations

from Owen in this section are from this chapter.

85. Gregory, Book XXXI, Ch. 45.88.

86. For more on the warning passages in Hebrews and the related issues of apostasy, perseverance, and assurance, see my book *Active Spirituality: Grace and Effort in the Christian Life* (Shepherd Press, 2014), especially pages 37-47, 93-96, and 113-127. My thinking has been profoundly shaped by the groundbreaking work of Thomas R. Schreiner and Ardel B. Caneday in *The Race Set Before Us: A Biblical Theology of Perseverance & Assurance* (IVP Academic, 2001).

87. J. Vernon McGee, *Thru the Bible: Matthew through Romans* (HarperCollins, 1983) pp 433-434.

88. D. Martyn Lloyd-Jones, *Spiritual Depression: Its Causes and Cure* (Eerdmans, 1965). This and the other quotations and references to Lloyd-Jones are from Chapter XIV.

89. DeYoung, p 97. Emphasis original.

90. John Owen, *The Works of John Owen*, vol. 6 (The Banner of Truth Trust, 1966) pp 567-568.

91. John Bunyan, *The Pilgrim's Progress* (The Banner of Truth Trust, 1977), pp 40-45. I have updated the spelling and punctuation to modern standards.

92. Graham, p 103.

93. Gregory, Book XXXI, Ch. 45.88.

94. DeYoung, p 100.

95. Graham, p 110-111.

96. Adapted from an account told by Ravi Zacharias, "Pleasure in the Balance" (*A Slice of Infinity*, 7-29-2002).

97. Peter Kreeft, *Back to Virtue* (Ignatius Press, 1992) p 112.

98. Lewis, *Mere Christianity*, pp 136-137.

99. Jeremiah Burroughs, *The Rare Jewel of Christian Contentment* (The Banner of Truth Trust, 1964) p 19.

100. Corrie Ten Boom, *The Hiding Place* (Minneapolis, MN: World Wide Publications, 1971) pp 198-199, 208-209.

101. Burroughs, p 29.

102. Lloyd-Jones, p 299. I owe the insights of this paragraph on this passage to Lloyd-Jones. See chapter XXI.

103. John Newton, "How Tedious and Tasteless the Hours," 1779.

104. See Tim Chester, *A Meal with Jesus: Discovering Grace, Community & Mission around the Table* (Crossway, 2011) and Craig L. Blomberg, *Contagious Holiness: Jesus' meals with sinners* (InterVarsity Press, 2005).

105. Quoted in Schimmel, p 142.

106. Frederick Buechner, quoted in DeYoung, 139.

107. Mabray, pp 97-98.

108. C. S. Lewis, *The Lion, the Witch, and the Wardrobe* (Macmillan Books, 1950) pp 32-33, 38. Emphasis added in the final quote.

109. Saint Augustine, *Teaching Christianity*, Trans. Edmund Hill (New City Press, 1996) p 108. For the whole discussion, see especially Book 1.3-4.

110. DeYoung, *Glittering Vices*, pp 152-153.

111. Thomas Aquinas, *Summa Theologica*, II-II. Q. 148. Art. 4, Translated by Fathers of the English Dominican Province (Coyote Canyon Press, Kindle Edition, 2010).

112. C. S. Lewis, *The Screwtape Letters* (HarperCollins, 1942, 2001) Letter 17.

113. See also verses 41, 48, 50, and 58.

114. John Piper, *A Hunger for God: Desiring God through Fasting and Prayer* (Crossway, 1997), p 23.

115. Bernard of Clairvaux, "Jesus, Thou Joy of Loving Hearts," 12th century; translated into English by Ray Palmer, 1858.

116. Geoffrey B. Wilson, *1 Corinthians: A Digest of Reformed Comment* (The Banner of Truth Trust, 1978) p 92.

117. Lewis, *The Great Divorce*, p 100.

118. Lewis, *Mere Christianity*, pp 104-105.

119. Sayers, *The Whimsical Christian: 18 Essays*, p 158.

120. Albert Camus, *The Fall*, Trans. by Justin O'Brien, (Vintage Books, 1956, 1991) p 102.

121. Augustine, *The Confessions*, Book VIII, Ch. 5,10, pp 192-193.

122. Plantinga, p 147.

123. C. S. Lewis, *The Pilgrim's Regress* (Eerdmans, 1958) pp 188-189.

124. Gregory, Book XXXI, Ch. 45.88.

125. Martin Luther, *Commentary on Galatians*, Trans. by Theodore Graebner, (Public Domain, Kindle Edition) Comments on Galatians 1:4.

126. From an old hymn, as quoted by Timothy J. Keller, *Gospel Christianity, Leader's Guide, Course 3* (Redeemer Presbyterian Church, 2007) p 49.

127. Lewis, *The Collected Letters of C. S. Lewis*, Volume II, p 391. Lewis was actually quoting Denis De Rougement and applying the concept to art.

128. Lewis, *Mere Christianity*, p 48.

129. Timothy J Keller, in his sermon, "Purity with Passion," 4/1/1990.

130. Lewis, *The Great Divorce*, p 46. The rest of the quotations at the end of this chapter are from chapter 11, pp 106-114.

Licensed to Kill
A Field Manual for Mortifying Sin

by Brian G. Hedges

**Your soul is a war zone.
Know your enemy.
Learn to fight.**

101 pp. Learn more at bit.ly/L2Kill

"A faithful, smart, Word-centered guide."
    – *Wes Ward, Revive Our Hearts*

"Are there things you hate that you end up doing anyway? Have you tried to stop sinning in certain areas of your life, only to face defeat over and over again? If you're ready to get serious about sin patterns in your life—ready to put sin to death instead of trying to manage it—this book outlines the only strategy that works. This is a book I will return to and regularly recommend to others."
    Bob Lepine, Co-Host, **FamilyLife Today**

"Brian Hedges shows the importance of fighting the sin that so easily entangles us and robs us of our freedom, by fleeing to the finished work of Christ every day. Well done!"
    Tullian Tchividjian, Coral Ridge Presbyterian Church; author, **Jesus + Nothing = Everything**

"Rather than aiming at simple moral reformation, *Licensed to Kill* aims at our spiritual transformation. Like any good field manual, this one focuses on the most critical information regarding our enemy, and gives practical instruction concerning the stalking and killing of sin. This is a theologically solid and helpfully illustrated book that holds out the gospel confidence of sin's ultimate demise."
    Joe Thorn, pastor and author, **Note to Self: The Discipline of Preaching to Yourself**

The Most Encouraging Book on Hell Ever

by Thor Ramsey

The biblical view of hell is under attack. But if hell freezes over, we lose a God of love and holiness, the good new of Jesus Christ, and more. / This book was written because hell glorifies God.

97 pages
Learn more at bit.ly/HELLBOOK

"Is the fear of God merely an Old-Testament doctrine? Does hell glorify God? Will we party with Pol Pot, Vlad the Impaler, Stalin, the Marquis de Sade, and Satan in heaven? And what about Bill Maher? For answers to these and other questions, this thought-provoking, bracing corrective to the soapy bromides of recent volumes on this subject may be just the ticket. And have we mentioned that it's entertaining and encouraging?"

> **Eric Metaxas, *New York Times* Best-selling author of**
> **Bonhoeffer: Pastor, Martyr, Prophet, Spy**

"*The Most Encouraging Book on Hell Ever* is also one of the wisest. This book is crammed with hilarious quips, but the message is deadly serious. Losing the doctrine of hell isn't trivial. It means losing truth, righteousness, and grace. Ultimately it means losing God. Thor's book uses humor to disarm readers just enough to deliver this crucial and timely message."

> **Drew Dyck, managing editor of Leadership Journal, a**
> **Christianity Today *publication***

""Praise God for Thor! The end must be getting near as Christians are actually getting funny. After a few pages, you'll realize this ain't your grandma's book about hell... but she'd love it just the same. Because it's only funny in the right places."

> **Stephen Baldwin, actor, author, radio host**

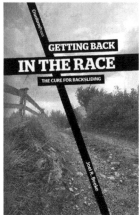

Getting Back in the Race
The Cure for Backsliding

by Joel R. Beeke

Backsliding is the worst thing that can happen to anyone claiming faith in Jesus.

Find out why. Learn the diagnosis. Experience the cure.

99 pp.
Learn more at bit.ly/THERACE

"This book is a masterpiece, and I do not say that lightly. This excellent work, so helpfully spiced with quotations from the Puritans, needs to be read over and over again. I heartily commend it."
Martin Holdt, Pastor; editor, Reformation Africa South

"Joel Beeke's characteristic clarity, biblical fidelity, and unflinching care as to detail and pastoral wisdom is obvious on every page. This book is an honest and sometimes chilling exposition of the seriousness of backsliding; at the same time, it unfailingly breathes the air of grace and hope. Timely and judicious."
Derek W. H. Thomas, First Presbyterian Church, Columbia, SC; Editorial Director, Alliance of Confessing Evangelicals

"'Don't settle for being a spiritual shrimp,' argues Dr. Beeke. The pity is that too many modern Christians are opting for shrimpishly small degrees of grace. Indwelling sin drags the careless believer down into guilty backsliding. This book is a prescription for the believer who feels his guilt."
Maurice Roberts, former editor, Banner of Truth *magazine*

"Dr. Beeke outlines the best means of bringing balm and healing to the backslidden soul. Highly recommended."
Michael Haykin, Professor, Southern Baptist Theo. Sem.

Knowable Word

Helping Ordinary People Learn
to Study the Bible

by Peter Krol
Foreword by Tedd Tripp

**Observe...Interpret...Apply. Simple
concepts at the heart of good Bible
study. Learn the basics in a few
minutes—gain skills for a lifetime.
The spiritual payoff is huge.
Ready?**

117 pages
Learn more at bit.ly/Knowable

"*Knowable Word* is valuable for those who have never done in-depth
Bible study and a good review for those who have. I look forward to
using this book to improve my own Bible study....a great service."
Jerry Bridges, author and speaker

"It is hard to over-estimate the value of this tidy volume. It is clear and
uncomplicated. No one will be off-put by this book. It will engage the
novice and the serious student of Scripture. It works as a solid read
for individuals or as an exciting study for a small group."
Tedd Tripp, pastor and author (from the Foreword)

"At the heart of *Knowable Word* is a glorious and crucial conviction:
that understanding the Bible is not the preserve of a few, but the
privilege and joy of all God's people. Peter Krol's book demystifies
the process of reading God's Word and in so doing enfranchises the
people of God. I warmly encourage you to read it. Better still, read it
with others and apply its method together."
Dr. Tim Chester, The Porterbrook Network

"Here is an excellent practical guide to interpreting the Bible. Krol has
thought through, tested, and illustrated in a clear, accessible way basic steps in interpreting the Bible, and made everything available in a
way that will encourage ordinary people to deepen their own study."
Vern Poythress, Westminster Theological Seminary

Contend
Defending the Faith in a Fallen World

by Aaron Armstrong

Every generation must contend for the faith.

We don't want to miss the mark.

Be merciful. Be uncompromising.

Contend!

91 pp.
Learn more at bit.ly/CONTEND

"Exactly the kind of book the church needs in our moment. We are tempted today on every side to be meek as a mouse. Armstrong's gospel-saturated writing, coupled with deeply instructive practical examples, will equip the church to be as bold as a lion, and to roar as Luther, Calvin, Spurgeon and Machen before us."
Owen Strachan, Assistant Professor, Boyce College

"Here is a balanced and passionate appeal, especially to young people, to take seriously their commitment to Jesus in all areas of life, both individually and in community, contending for the Faith, using both their minds and their hearts in defense of the Truth, in the manner laid out by the apostle Jude. May this call be heard far and wide."
Dr. Peter Jones, Executive Director, truthXchange

"A fine combination of concise biblical exposition, down-to-earth examples, contemporary illustrations, and challenging practical application. It's not only an ideal book for discipling a new believer, but also for shaking the more mature out of dangerous complacency and passivity."
David P. Murray, Puritan Reformed Theological Seminary

"Helps us understand why it's hard to take a stand, what's worth fighting for, and how to do it. I'm grateful for this biblical and helpful book."
Darryl Dash, Pastor and blogger at Dashhouse.com

Made in the USA
Middletown, DE
30 April 2015